A Witch Wins
JUSTICE

A MEMOIR OF VICTORY WORTHY OF A WITCH

By Joey Piscitelli

2012

Copyright © 2011 Joey Piscitelli
All rights reserved.

Cover Art : "Lady Justice"
Original acrylic painting by James Piscitelli -
jamespiscitelliart.com - Dec 2011

ISBN: 1463672128
ISBN 13: 9781463672126

CONTENTS

Introduction 1
Before the Beginning – A Prior Lifetime. 5
Timelessness Interrupted. 7
The Early Catholic Years. 11
Into the Salesian High School of Horrors. 53
After the Molester Disappeared 99
Collecting Books and Learning. 133
Reconstructing my Reincarnation 147
Into the Millennium 153
Letter to Ratzinger. 171
The Court Trial 185
Magickal Interference 225
How I Used Magick to Win the Case 231
Acknowledgements. 239
References. 245

Definition: "Magick"
Magick is the science or art of causing change to occur with will". It is usually described to define an occult art. This spelling is used to differentiate it from the word "Magic," which is associated with the stage art of slight of hand.

"In memory of all the millions of innocent Witches that were tortured and killed by the Catholic Church, because of religious prejudice and intolerance."

- STREGA VIOLA - COVEN OF THE PURPLE WITCH

"In memory of all the millions of innocent children that were abused and molested by Catholic clergy."

- JOEY PISCITELLI

Introduction

The story I present to you is nonfiction. It is my story. Throughout history, there have been countless tortures, killings, abuses, and atrocities that have been sanctioned and committed by Roman Catholic hierarchy and its underlying clergy, supposedly in the name of God. The Catholic Church, and related members and constituents, massacred, killed, and burned hundreds of thousands of men, women, and children accused of witchcraft or suspected of being "witches." Many of the victims were not witches; many were merely pagans, unfortunate scapegoats, or children.

But many victims were in fact witches.

The Catholic Church also continued the abuse, rape, and molestation of tens of thousands of innocent children for hundreds of years, and has recently paid out over a billion dollars in legal settlements for sexual abuse of children in California alone. Thousands of victims have sued the Catholic Church in recent decades, and I was one of those abuse victims who sued the Church when the California legislature enacted a law to allow former victims to file suit to seek justice in 2003. Most of the lawsuits filed against the Catholic Church in California, over 99 percent, were settled out of court.

Approximately only one dozen cases of Catholic clergy molestation lawsuit cases in the United States, including California, ever went to jury trial, and my suit was one of them.

A Witch Wins JUSTICE

I filed suit against the Catholic Church, Rev. Stephen Whelan, and the Salesian Order of Roman Catholic priests.

I am also a practicing witch and a non-Satanist, and I am considered an earth-based pagan.

I am the only molestation victim to have ever gone to a jury trial in Contra Costa County, California, against a clergy abuser of the church. I am also the only clergy abuse victim to have ever won a court jury trial against the church in US history, with no tangible evidence or documentation.

In addition, I am the only practicing witch in world history to have ever defeated the Catholic Church in a jury trial whatsoever.

According to the Population Reference Bureau, it is estimated that currently there are 7 billion people on the Planet Earth. It is also estimated that the world population since the beginning of creation is 108 billion people. This would mean that I am the only witch out of 108 billion people to have ever defeated the Roman Catholic Church in a jury trial.

I also believe that I am a reincarnated witch, and the dreams/memories I recalled as a two- and three-year-old confirm my conviction and belief of my prior life. I am convinced that the law of Karma dictates the outcome of our lives and predetermines our destiny. I believe we are here to learn lessons and that we are all indiscriminately and atomically connected to the universe. I further believe that we are a product of the causes and effects of universally shared energy. I do not believe in the Biblical definition of a witch, or the Christian invention

Introduction

of the definition of a witch as "a person who has a pact with the devil," as I do not believe in the existence of the devil, nor in the existence of hell. It is my position that real witches traditionally were, and still are, herbalists, nature lovers and worshipers, wise women and men, healers, and spiritual beings, just for examples—but not devil worshipers.

The irony of my legal case reveals itself in the person of Cardinal William Levada, then Archbishop of San Francisco, and now the Vatican's Grand Inquisitor, whom I personally battled with for several years. Cardinal Levada was promoted by the Pope in 2005 to be the "Prefect for the Congregation of the Doctrine of the Faith," formerly known as "The Office of the Inquisition." To continue the tale of irony, at the time I filed suit against the Catholic Church for molesting me as an adolescent, the priest who molested me was working for Cardinal Levada in San Francisco as an Associate Pastor at St. Peter and Paul's Cathedral in San Francisco's North Beach District. My battle was literally at the Inquisitor General's front door.

It is estimated conservatively that the Salesians of San Francisco, directly employed and chosen by Cardinal Levada, who had retained several law firms to represent them against me in court, paid out several million dollars in attorney fees to ensure an absolute victory in court. The litigation lasted five years.

It was inevitable that a reincarnated witch would return at some point in time to seek justice against the Catholic Church, given the sheer numbers of those that were abused, and the law of chances. My story is a

A Witch Wins JUSTICE

true account of my life, the subsequent introduction of trauma, and my perception of the sometimes-inexplicable blend of magick, mystery, and the cause and effect of timelessness and destiny. This is not a story of revenge; it is a story of deserved justice, and the laws of Karma.

—Joey Piscitelli, 2012

Thus I came to a deep religiosity, which, however, came to an abrupt end at the age of twelve. Through the reading of popular scientific books, I soon reached a conviction that much in the stories of the Bible could not be true...suspicion against every kind of authority grew out of this experience, an attitude that has never left me.

—Albert Einstein

Before the Beginning: A Prior Lifetime

I told the interrogators I did not have a pact with the devil, yet they kept torturing me. I couldn't tolerate the pain. Then everything changed. I have a faint memory of those women dressed in black; they looked over me as I lay there. I thought I had just closed my eyes, but I don't think that's what really happened. I've never seen darkness like this before. There's nothing left to worry about, and the darkness is peaceful. I do not know how long I have been in this place, but I don't even care. There's nobody else around, and I don't care about that either. I'm not lonely, or hungry. I don't think I am tired, but I feel as though I will go to sleep, although there's nothing about me that would need rest. I know the things I used to care about are gone, and I realize that I won't miss them, I just need to float through the darkness. I used to think things...that seem to be fading away, and I'm not worried about trying to remember what they were. I don't think that anything at all matters, and I've forgotten for the most part who I am, or where I came from.

There is no one to answer to, and no one to worry about. That feeling must be different from what I used to feel. I am sure that if I fade away everything will be as it is supposed to be, and there is a reason why I can't remember what has happened. The only thing that I can remember well is that this has happened before, and I will wake from the darkness, and there will be something to learn. But what makes me feel that way is unknown. All of what I have now are feelings of the unknown; I only possess the need to drift through space. Perhaps I am asleep, and when I come to realization again, I will forget the darkness, and I will care about who I was, or where I have been. But I don't know if that is true. I do not know how I have the ability to think these words. I may have learned that somehow.

I do have the feeling that I was somewhere else, or I was someone. But what is someone? I don't know what someone is. There are so many things that I feel I have forgotten, and I think I would remember them if I wanted to. But I don't want to remember them now ; it wouldn't be right. And this darkness and peacefulness was not always with me, but I need to fade away.

I am one with darkness and peace.

If I don't see you no more in this world, I'll see you in the next one...and don't be late.

—JIMI HENDRIX, "VOODOO CHILD" (1968)

Timelessness Interrupted

The silence and peacefulness does not feel the same. I feel as though I will see things, things that I know are distressing; and there is a somewhat familiar, disturbing sound in the distance. I do not feel comfortable anymore. I must have been asleep, or unconscious, and perhaps I dreamed of dying? I feel I'm going to open my eyes, and I know I will not like where I am. How did I get here, and what is this place?

Now I can see a blurry vision: there is a man pointing at me, and I am in a room with many other people, and I do not recognize them. Or do I? The room is becoming more clear to me, and I am sitting on a chair, next to a judge. There is a jury to my right, and there are many lawyers in the room. I can't be here. This must be the dream, or the nightmare. I know I wasn't here minutes ago; I should wake up from this horror, and go back to the peacefulness. I do not want to be in this courtroom. It's too frightful.

But the man staring at me is relentless. I just heard him say something, but I don't quite understand what it was; perhaps he was trying to trick me. I heard someone call

A Witch Wins JUSTICE

him Mr. Mason, and he seems to be very evil to me. He's shouting now...

"DO YOU BELIEVE IN OUR LORD JESUS CHRIST?"

I can't talk. I need to escape.

He shouts again, "DO YOU BELIEVE IN OUR LORD JESUS CHRIST?"

The room is spinning, and I can't hear very well; the courtroom is getting foggy, and darker, and I am floating out of the witness stand, and toward the ceiling, and no one is aware of it. But where am I going?

I can't see anything, or hear anything at all. Perhaps I am going to the peaceful place, where there is eternal silence.

But now something strange is happening; I can feel things again. Painful things. Very painful things...heat. It's very hot, unbelievably hot, and I can smell smoke. I can barely see once more, and I feel intense horrible pain. What is this place? Now I remember.

I'm in a fire. I am tied to a post, and I am in a fire. There are flames engulfing me, and my flesh is peeling off of me. There are people from the church staring at me, and yelling those familiar words again.

"DO YOU BELIEVE IN OUR LORD JESUS CHRIST?"

I can't take the pain anymore, and I am starting to float again, out of the fire and away from the evil people who are watching me burn. It's becoming dark again, and I can hear women whispering to each other, but I can not see them.

I do not think I can remember who I am anymore, and the women keep whispering. I don't feel the pain of the heat. I must have disappeared from the fire somehow. But where am I?

Timelessness Interrupted

I can barely hear one of the women whisper now, ever so faintly,

"Someone is going to tell the story?"

What story is she talking about? The voices are getting harder to hear, and the darkness is surrounding me. I'm disappearing once more, and the last words I hear are "the story." I do not know "a story," and I do not feel anything anymore. I'm back to the peaceful, quiet, dark place.

I feel I'm traveling somewhere, and I'm beginning once again to forget everything, and the past is fading away. Someone is going to tell a story....

The Early Catholic Years

This incarnation began, I believe, when I had realized I kept hearing the name "Joey" whenever my Mommy or Daddy would call me or pick me up. I don't know how I learned to talk this language; it just occurred somehow. Mommy and Daddy must have taught me how to talk and who I am. It just happened, and I am not sure of how it happened, but here I am.

Sam and Chick, my Mommy and Daddy, must have taught me quite a bit. It just took a couple of years, but it stuck. We lived in Richmond, California, I would hear them say, and we came from Brooklyn, New York. I was three, they would tell people, my brother was four, and my sister was two. I recognized those numbers; I heard them all the time. Two, three, and four.

They also told me we were Catholic and we were Italian. I could say the words back to them, and they were proud. They said they were so happy I could walk and talk so well at such an early age. The calendar in the kitchen with Jesus on it displayed the year 1958. I soaked up everything they told me like a sponge, because that's what toddlers do, but I did not have the capacity to understand why. It just was that way. Whatever they said to me I kept and I remembered—there was lot's of room in the storage cells in my little head. They never said there was another religion besides the Catholic Religion, but I learned that later in school. I accepted the fact that I was Catholic, just like I accepted that the numbers and the alphabet Mommy taught me were real, and there was never a reason to consider otherwise. I wasn't exactly sure what religion was, but it had something to do with God, and with the church we went to on Sundays.

They showed me pictures of God, and Mary, and tried to explain that He made me, and that He made the whole world. It never occurred to me to think that God may not be there, or to question where I came from; those were things a three-year-old didn't ponder—even a three-year-old that was as smart as they told me I was.

I believed everything I was told, and everything was taken for granted—like the cross on the wall, the picture of Jesus in the living room, or the statue of Mary on the dresser. As a matter of fact, I think at least one wall in every room in the house had a picture of Jesus or another religious icon somewhere in it. Jesus was everywhere, and my parents were sure to remind me of that.

But I used to stare at the Crucifix of Jesus on the wall, and it was odd that it seemed so familiar. I couldn't tell if he was sleeping, or if he was in pain. And I did not know why he was hung on the wooden cross like that, or why Mommy and Daddy would want him hanging around like that, with almost no clothes on. I felt like I was sure I recognized him though, as if I had seen him somewhere else in the world, but not at church. It was eerie, but acceptable. I couldn't analyze at that age. I just dismissed things easily, as toddlers do. I liked my world. I didn't have to figure out how to survive; Mommy and Daddy did that for me.

The Early Catholic Years

The world was a fine place, an organized place, but most of all, a secure place.

A Catholic place. Mommy, Daddy, Jesus, God, and Mary. It was all so good. I had trust in all of them, and I believed they had trust in me. There was no such thing as death, poison, hate, child abuse, or any negative threats in my life; that is, at least when I was awake. I was completely unaware that any of those things even existed in the world around me. I would continue to believe this for years, as long as God was watching over me. And I knew it was true, that he watched carefully over me, because Mommy had told me that same story so many times, and He was in so many rooms.

As a bright three-year-old, I was able to remember almost everything, and my aunts and uncles were amazed.

"What a memory that kid has," they would say, and it made me so content.

But then they would whisper their dark observations to Mommy, thinking I couldn't hear them.

"Where does he get all those weird stories?" my aunt would ask.

"I don't know," Mommy would defend me. "Kids just have such an imagination."

But I could tell Mommy looked worried.

The memories and "imagination" may have been a gift, but also a curse.

I remembered things that the other kids didn't remember, things that Mommy or Daddy didn't teach me. Some of them were beautiful and virtually indescribable, but some of them were facts I should not have known.

There was no source from where I could have accessed the information.

In my earliest years, I had this wonderful recollection of a recurring dream of floating through a dark night full of stars, and I was looking down from high above...at myself, far below. Then I would slowly descend downwards, and float around in the area of what seemed to be the bright kitchen ceiling. I would then look down at a thin white table with white linens and see myself on the table, looking back at me.

This scene would morph into the feeling that I was on the table, looking back up at myself floating on the ceiling. But the sight was too difficult to look up at, because there was such a brilliant light that I was unable to look at it for more than a second. I thought it was like looking at the sun. At this point the scene would turn dark, as if I had to close my eyes from the brilliance, and then the dream would fade away.

I had this dream constantly from the age of two to about the age of seven. I would try to describe it to my mother, a task too difficult to explain articulately, but she said she understood that I was dreaming of flying and floating, and told me not to worry about it, that it was normal.

The most interesting thing about the dream was that as I was floating through the dark night full of stars, I realized I had no arms or legs, or any body parts to speak of. I felt no pain, no heat, and no cold, and had no sense of smell or sound. It's incomprehensible for a two- or three-year-old to explain or understand that your brain is inside your head, and your body is controlled by your brain, but I knew I floated somehow without my body.

The Early Catholic Years

I just plain existed.

Many nights as I went to bed, I would look at the sheetrock wall adjacent to the right side of my bed, and there was an odd-shaped piece of texture on the wall that resembled a small child curled up in a ball, similar to a fetal position. As I dozed off, this image would send me into the atmosphere, looking down at myself in the far distance below.

I had the sensation that I was simply energy, but I had no means to compare this feeling to any other sensation I was familiar with when I was awake. Perhaps, I thought, that's what dreams are made of; it's just you floating. I loved having that floating dream, and it made me feel safe for some reason, even though I did not understand it; and sometimes I felt cheated when I woke from it, because I never got to see the end of the dream, or where it had actually started, but I knew a large part of it was missing.

It wasn't until years later that it suddenly dawned on me that it could have been a dream of a birth memory; that the ceiling in the bright kitchen was actually a hospital delivery room, and I was remembering being born. Whatever the case, the dream has always given me a reason to ponder what exists beyond this life. An important aspect of the dream of floating in the atmosphere was also the sensation of "timelessness."

I will refer to this sensation later, as it is probably one of the most important sensations of the practice of Magick, which I refer to as the "absence of time."

This out-of-body experience I recalled as a child was much clearer to decipher as I grew older. I finally discovered over thirty years later that the dream of floating, which I believe was actually a memory, has parallels with disassociation, and it is a defense mechanism that your mind may use to escape certain unwanted situations.

It was also similar to trauma, or some types of trance—things I was not aware of at the time. But I had other recurring dreams or nightmares as a very young child, continuing into kindergarten and first grade. Dreams I was horrified of, and ashamed of; dreams that were haunting.

The world I loved so much as an active child had an opposite and unwanted twist; it was the world I sometimes experienced during sleep. I can recall one particular persistent dream about a stone building with large twisted, splintered timbers in the ceilings and walls, timbers that smelled of smoke. My Daddy smoked cigarettes, and I was familiar with the smell of smoke in a room, and I had wondered if the smoke had seeped into the dreams somehow at night. I would fall asleep sometimes and drift into the enjoyment of the surrealistic dream of floating, when the smoke and the begrimed stone building would slowly creep into the scene.

Then suddenly there I was, shaking with fear in the cold stone room, looking up at those brown, twisted beams, being inundated with the malodor of that awful smoke. The smoke was coming from somewhere below, drifting upward from some kind of ash on the filthy floor.

Brisk flashes of toothless, wrinkled men with dirty clothes and twine ropes would whiz past my limited field of vision, and a morbid stench I could not identify would fill the room. It wasn't smoke, it was exceedingly worse. Then came the screaming. It wasn't like my little sister's screaming; it was considerably louder, and longer, and

The Early Catholic Years

it came from somewhere in the stone room. It echoed throughout the room, a shrieking horror that filled my ears without mercy. Although I resisted, I would strain to see where the screams came from, but I realized I couldn't move.

My hands were bound, and the sense of fright would creep over me, and I felt myself trying to wake up out of the nightmare, but I couldn't. I could hear myself moan, and then came the wet salt.

That's what it was.

It would always save me. I could feel the wet salt roll down my face, from my eyes, and it would slowly seep down into the side of my mouth, as I was moaning in the dark, and it would wake me up.

Thank you God, for the salt.

I loved the wet salt. I still do. And I always will.

After the wet salt would wake me, I would push my plaid blanket aside, roll out of my tiny bed, and run into Mommy's room. I thanked God again that she was always there. I always tapped her shoulder with my hand, still wet from wiping the salty tears, and she would eventually wake up.

"Joey," she would say sleepily, her eyes half-closed, "did you have one of those nightmares again?"

"Mommy," I would cry back, "I was in that room again, the one with the ropes and smoke."

She would always calm me down and take me back to bed, assuring me that it was just a dream. But when she went back to her room, I could hear my father ask if I had one of those nightmares again.

"Where the hell is he getting that from?" he would ask.

"I don't know," she would answer. "it doesn't seem normal."

I thought they were right. No one else had the nightmares. Just Joey. Some nights were peaceful, and I floated throughout the dreams like a bird, and all would seem to go back to being beautiful.

But then came the fires. The goddamned fires.

All of a sudden, out of nowhere, there I would be again. Only now, I was outside the stone building. At first I thought there were clouds all over the sky, but they weren't really clouds. And the smoke was burning my eyes this time. I couldn't see well. There was too much of a blur, but flames would intermittently light up my face, and the heat would rise and creep up to me. I couldn't move again, and the smoke seemed to fill my lungs. It was hard to breathe. The clouds were getting thicker by the second.

Someone was screaming. I tried to see who it was, and a horrible sense of doom consumed me. It was me screaming. I was in the fire. I tried to wake out of it, but I couldn't.

So I waited for the salt. I kept waiting.

But the saltwater wouldn't roll down my face to save me. It was too hot. The fire dried it too fast. I was melting. God, why didn't Mommy and Daddy hear me screaming?

They just couldn't. The snapping and crackling of the fire was too loud. I kept melting. But then I noticed the fire didn't make anymore sound. I couldn't feel myself melting. That was odd. It didn't hurt. There was no pain, no sound, and no smell. Just like in the kitchen ceiling.

The Early Catholic Years

I could feel myself rising up out of the fire, and I was floating again. It was a relief to be able to float away from the fire, the smoke, and the screaming. Then came the dark night full of stars again. I didn't need the salt this time. It was okay now. The dark night was beautiful, and I would slowly head back to the ceiling.

In the morning I would tell Mommy about the fires. She would always stare at me; I learned later it wasn't a stare full of pity. It was a stare of fright. I scared Mommy with the fire stories. My mother did not know how to address the issue of the fire stories, as I had no experience with seeing a fire, or burning, and I had not been exposed to discussions of any witch burnings, or tortures of any kind.

We didn't even have a TV then. After listening to my tales of these nightmares, my mother would tell my father it was OK.

"It's just a phase he's going through," she would say. "He'll be OK."

I didn't know what a phase was, but I was hoping she was right. Mommy was always right. And the phase had almost ended—the fire dreams seemed to be coming to a halt several months later.

I remember Mommy telling Daddy she asked the doctor why I dreamed of being tied up in fires, and the doctor asked if I had been in a fire anywhere. Mommy said no, that I had never seen one, and the doctor said it was very strange. It worried her even more.

As the fire dreams began to subside, the new dreams started. They seemed to be out of order. It must have been before the fires. It felt like it. I don't know why, but it felt like it. Just like before, I would be sleeping calmly, and then I would be back at the stone building. But it

A Witch Wins JUSTICE

was different, it didn't smell as bad, and there were other glimpses of men who I did not recognize. Men with robes. Men with books. They were mad and mean. They yelled about God, and I didn't understand them. Their words were not making any sense; some of the words sounded like they were from a different language.

They hated me, I knew that; but I didn't know why. I just wanted to leave and go home. They screamed about Jesus Christ. I could see the man at the big wooden box—he kept yelling, shaking his book, and looking up at the ceiling screaming about Jesus over and over. I looked up at the ceiling, I couldn't see anything. Just more twisted beams. What was he looking at? He spit while he screamed, and his face was red; I could see his veins popping out of his skin in his head. He disgusted me with his anger.

Then came the toothless men with the ropes that stank. They tied me up.

I started to moan when it hurt, and I waited for the salt. The wet salt came for me this time, maybe because there was no fire yet. I couldn't wait to taste it again. The salt saved me, and I was able to leave the room with the angry man who screamed about Jesus Christ. I would go back to Mommy's room to tell her about it. The next morning I would go into the kitchen and make sure the saltshaker was on the table. I always asked Mommy to keep it full. I knew as long as I ate salt everyday, it would save me at night. Mommy never knew why, but she kept the saltshaker filled for me. I put plenty of salt on all of my food. I still do.

These dreams did not happen after I had learned or heard information beforehand about any of the

The Early Catholic Years

occurrences that were in the nightmares, from any person or film, or any story anyone read or related to me. I wish they would have. Then it would have made sense. Then Mommy wouldn't have been so scared.

Every night before I went to bed, I would say my night prayers, which consisted of an "Our Father" and a "Hail Mary." I think I preferred the Hail Mary, because I thought she was cool, being Jesus' mom; and she dressed real nice, looked good in her blue veil, and appeared to be so loving. A perfect Mom. The night prayer would end when my dad or mom would say, "Say goodnight to DeeDee."

I would say, "Goodnight Mommy, goodnight Daddy, goodnight Deedee."

I never knew why my mom and dad referred to God as Deedee—maybe it was cute baby talk, or an Italian thing; but whatever the case, I dropped the Deedee thing at about age six. I outgrew it.

I was old enough to call God his real name, which was "God." It was about the time that I was around six that I realized that as long as I knew God so personally, mainly because I said my night prayers every night, that nothing bad could ever happen to me. I felt very secure about being in his hands and in the hands of my parents.

God and I were very tight then. I knew that he must have helped me wake up from the bad dreams, and I knew he would always take care of me. As a matter of fact, my mom and dad verified that on several occasions.

"God will always take care of you," they would say, "as long as you say your prayers and go to church every Sunday."

A Witch Wins JUSTICE

It was very reassuring, the whole God thing, but it had a catch. Because as my parents would always remind me, "He's always watching everything you do." That's the tradeoff, I had decided, so I knew I wasn't going to be able to get away with too much crap, but I would always be protected, and most importantly—and this was the big deal—I would go to "heaven."

Now this realization gave me mixed emotions because, as I understood it, you go to heaven after you die. Of course heaven has got to be the ultimate place to end up, but who wants to die to get there? At that time though, luckily, I didn't know any dead people, and nobody in my family was going to die anyway. So dying wasn't anything to worry about, especially if you went to Catholic Church every Sunday. In addition, I did not really know what death was at that age; the closest interpretive assumption I could make was that it was like sleeping.

But every once in a while, when I heard the word "death," I had an odd feeling that I had heard it somewhere years ago, and it bothered me that I could not remember where. Sometimes I wondered if any of my dreams had anything to do with death, but I decided they couldn't have, because I still didn't know any dead people. So as kids do, I dismissed it, possibly because I couldn't deal with it, or maybe because it was a product of childhood resilience. I was more concerned with Catholic Church service.

Catholic Church "service" was a real mystery, although I always took it for granted that the majority of the world's population was also Catholic and that everybody shared and accepted the "normality" of the

The Early Catholic Years

Catholic Sunday service. It was called "mass." It was held on Sundays, and the leaders of the mass were called "priests." These priests wore costumes, and the people in attendance got dressed up, women wore scarves on their heads, and everybody said prayers together. But the prayers were in a different language, which was Latin. I had no idea what *dominos vobiscum* meant, or if it was really important, but I could say it. And the incense they burned during the mass smelled really good. Something was familiar about the Latin language—it had a sound to it that reminded me somehow of the mean men in the nightmares who screamed about Jesus; I couldn't put it together.

One of the most interesting things to me was that during the sacrifice of the mass, a man walked down every aisle, and each person in the church pew put money into a basket he held in front of them. If someone didn't put money in the basket, it seemed to me that everybody looked at the cheapskate like he was an idiot. I know I did.

"A good Catholic always puts money in the basket," as the nuns always reminded us.

It was in 1961 that I entered the first grade at St. John's Catholic School in El Cerrito. And it was in the first grade that I was initially introduced to "nuns." They were also referred to as "Sisters." The nuns wore a black-and-white costume every day of the year, and I had imagined that they never removed their garments, even in the shower. Perhaps the garments were actually sown to their bodies; I never found out. Their veils covered their entire heads; I never knew why. These nuns were very smart and very powerful. One of my first grade teachers was

A Witch Wins JUSTICE

Sister Paul, which I immediately thought was strange, because I was under the impression that Paul was a boy's name at the time. I soon found out why she had a boy's name: because Sister Paul could kick anybody's ass. One word, one sound, any slight movement out of order, and not only was she there in a millisecond, but she had her wooden ruler out and it was down on your knuckles before you could say "Holy Shit." She was a superhuman who could see behind her veil when she had her back turned toward you, and I was convinced it was caused by a divine power given to nuns specifically by God.

But I found something else out in first grade. Sister Paul told me I was very advanced in reading and comprehension. No one had ever told me that before; momma just said I was smart. Where did that comprehension come from? Did it suddenly happen there in first grade, or was I advanced before that? Would it be safe to tell Sister Paul about all the weird dreams? I wondered if that would ruin her impression of me. If it scared Mommy, it must be something that was wrong with me. I decided not to tell her.

I found out I could draw fairly well, and that was a surprise also. I realized I had no idea who I really was or what I was capable of. And I wondered if it would continue, or if it was temporary.

I started to really like the school, and I found myself becoming proud and actually admiring Sister Paul. That is, until I experienced her dark side. One minute she was praising me and telling me I was brilliant, the next minute she was slapping me or hitting the top of my brilliant head with her knuckles.

The Early Catholic Years

What a teacher. What a nun. What a bitch.

The Sister Paul love-hate thing was overwhelming, but I found learning easy, and I do not ever remember having to put much effort into classwork, but I always got good grades. Actually I remember Sister Paul telling me that very thing.

"Joey," she said, "you don't ever seem to put much effort into classwork, but you do very well on tests. I could imagine what you could do if you really tried your hardest. You are a lucky boy."

She ended this inspirational pep talk with a firm backhand slap across my face. I figured at that time that this kind of "praise and strike" ritual must have been an Irish tradition of the nuns, and I should accept it as a common practice.

Regardless of her motives, that was the coolest thing that I have ever heard a nun say. It gave me a big head, but I still got my knuckles whacked by the ruler at least once a week. I began to notice I had a handicap of sorts; I was the smallest boy in the class. The others were beginning to call me "shrimp" and "pewee." I suddenly realized that size does matter, at least in grammar school. Not to worry, I thought, I would probably grow next year. But every year was the same; I was the smallest boy in the class.

My first introduction to the fact that there were other religions in the world was later on in first grade, when one nun revealed that "the Catholic religion is the one true religion."

I was stunned.

There were actually other religions? All of my relatives were practicing Catholics, most of them Italian, and it was never discussed by any family members I knew that there were other churches or faiths.

In addition to the nun revealing this alarming news that there were other religions in the world, I was introduced to a new surprise when the nun produced a little cardboard box on her desk. It was a yellow, octagonal cardboard box about six inches high and four inches across, with pictures on it.

The nun kept the little box on her desk in front of the class every day. She told the class that the box was a "Pagan box." There were pictures on the Pagan box that we assumed were pictures of actual Pagan babies and children.

The children looked like Eskimos to me, and one of the children looked like a little monkey with fangs. Some of the girls in the classroom could not look at the picture without cringing.

We were told to put money into the Pagan box as much as possible. I did not have the courage to ask the nun what a Pagan was, as it was so mysterious, and it was obvious to me at the time that she did not want to reveal the secret of what the Pagan box was for some reason.

Someone in the class finally asked the nun what a Pagan box was. The whole class was silent and in awe, and the nun took a deep breath and decided that it was time for us to hear the gruesome truth. The Sister was delighted to tell us exactly what a Pagan was. She tried to contain herself as she sternly explained it to us.

"Pagans are the ignorant people in this world who are not Catholics. They believe in false gods and worship demons and devils. They are the people like the Jews,

The Early Catholic Years

the Protestants, the Indians, and the like. They do not know any better."

Sister continued. "I want each one of you to try to place money in the Pagan box every day, to aid our missionaries, so that our missionaries can convert the ignorant Pagans into Catholics, so that their souls will be saved from burning in hell forever."

Several six-year-old jaws dropped simultaneously as the class heard this unbelievable horror. How could this world be so wicked? Not only were there ignorant savages in the world who were not Catholic, but they also worshiped devils and demons. This was a lot of information to take in at one time. I left class totally confused, but I did trust the nun and took her for her word. Why would she lie? She was, after all, a woman of God, and she was my teacher. And I was there to learn from her. She taught us Math, English, History, and other important subjects. I would never have questioned that anything she said could ever possibly be wrong. I would never question anyone in any position of authority; that kind of thinking was unknown to me completely.

What really bothered me was that the poor Pagans would burn in hell because they weren't baptized Catholic. Why? It didn't seem fair. Something was odd about this fact, and it troubled me. But I was not going to ask the reason, as I was too afraid to question the Sister's statements.

Sister Paul was sure to mention what good Catholics we were going to grow up to be, and how proud she was that we were learning to donate money at our age.

A Witch Wins JUSTICE

"It's only nickels and dimes now," she said. "But as you grow older you will surely be donating much, much more than that."

It was our early introduction to unselfishness. As one nun explained,

"Those who give the most to the Catholic Church are in line to go to heaven first."

And I also noticed that those who put more money in the Pagan baby box were sure to get "A"s in class, which must have been a coincidence, and there must be some kind of correlation between donating money and the resulting higher classroom performance. But this practice also seemed to be unfair, and nobody was questioning it. It seemed odd to me that I would get 100 percent on a spelling test and receive an A-, and another boy would get 75 percent on a spelling test and receive an A, after donating more money into the Pagan box than I did. Since silence is golden, I saved myself from the wrath of the wooden ruler by not bringing this subject to the attention of Sister Paul.

During the "Religion class" portion of grade school, we were also reminded constantly about how we were born sinners and saved by the blessed Sacrament of baptism. Some of the other important Catholic-school teaching examples we learned were as follows: "We are guilty as descendants of Adam and Eve."

"We are born sinners because of Original Sin."
"We will burn in hell if we are not baptized."
"Sex is filthy."
"All Pagans worship Satan."
"God is everywhere."
"The Catholic religion is the one true religion."

The Early Catholic Years

"All other religions are false, and their followers will rot in hell with the devil."

Apparently, as we learned, our earliest ancestors, Adam and Eve, dabbled too much into the forbidden fruit, with their naked bodies covered by giant leaves, and their abominable sin was passed on to us. Exactly what the abominable sin that Adam and Eve did to each other was left to our imagination, which of course, was a guilty imagination, as the nuns pointed out. We were told at the time that the dirty deeds committed by these two weak ancestors involved an apple, of all things, and a snake.

I remember turning red and shaking when she told us this, because that very day, I had an apple in my lunchbox. I couldn't stop thinking about it.

My mother never mentioned how evil it was. I was quiet as a nun told the class more details.

The fact that Eve "bit" the apple first, which was a grave and costly mistake and the whopper of all sins, was very disturbing. But then, to make it worse, she coerced Adam into biting the apple, which blew it for all of mankind. What a horrible, despicable couple they were. The nuns would wince with pain when telling us the story, which I believed took a lot of courage on their part.

This explains how we are all born with Adam and Eve's sin on our souls, which appropriately was called "Original Sin," the nuns assured us, but luckily baptism washed the degrading scars from our guilty souls. It appeared as though we were accessories after the fact, which was still a punishable crime.

Other children, who were not baptized Catholics, still had the Original Sin on their souls, which pretty much ensured a ticket directly to hell someday.

A Witch Wins JUSTICE

I couldn't wait until lunchtime to throw my apple away. I felt dirty thinking about it, and I had to go into the bathroom to wash my hands.

It suddenly occurred to me that I knew other kids who lived on my street that did not go to my Catholic School—like Donny, the boy who lived across the street, who went to a public school. I couldn't wait to ask him if he was Catholic and disclose what I had learned from the nuns. I'll never forget the day I got the courage to ask him.

"Are you Catholic?" I asked him with genuine concern.

"No," he answered. "Why?"

"Because you're going to burn in hell forever," I said with newly found wisdom.

Donny ran home crying, and his mother came over and chewed me out. I couldn't for the life of me figure out what her problem was—I was justified and correct, and they were potentially damned forever. It must be the sins on their souls causing their stupidity, I thought.

The concerned nuns reminded us repeatedly that if it were not for the holy Catholic priests who baptized us, we would have been surely damned.

I have to say that after having all these ideas tattooed on my brain by nuns who beat me constantly as a child, I had mixed feelings about my faith.

The classrooms and the church itself were riddled with icons and statues. As students we got used to seeing the icon of the crucified dead man on a cross, nailed and punctured, blood gushing from his torso, with a crown made of spikes on his skull. And this was supposed to be normal. But the marriage of gruesomeness and holiness was really an enigma.

The crucified man on the cross was Jesus Christ, the Son of God; and His mother, named Mary, was a virgin—not like other women, who were "with sin."

The nun was very staunch and adamant about Mary the mother of God being a virgin and her being chaste and pure, unlike other mothers. I had no idea what she was talking about. We were also taught that it was our fault that Christ died this way, by horrible crucifixion, because of our wicked and filthy sins. Apparently he died this way because of sins that everybody on earth before and after his life had committed or will commit.

Besides the negativity and guilt dished out to us daily at Catholic school, for being born sinners, there was also the weirdness and abnormal views about sex. Mostly there was an absence of discussion of the subject, and a taboo and mystery established about its existence.

The few references that I can remember pertaining to sex at all were when a nun would occasionally say that "sex was dirty" and "sex is sinful." The nuns were very specific mentioning that Mary the Mother of God conceived her Son Jesus without the filthy sin on her pure record.

The nuns unanimously shared the opinion that having a child was not possible without the nasty sinfulness attached to pregnancy, which was a horror that Mary had escaped from. I believe that the nuns were so immersed in the avoidance of the issue of sex that to them, the mere mention of the discussion in itself was capable of contaminating one's soul.

A Witch Wins JUSTICE

I had guessed that my mother was guilty of the sinfulness too, because the nuns told us that Mary the Mother of God was the only woman ever to pull off both the virgin and mother combo.

I was afraid to look at my mother for days, wondering what she had done.

I was embarrassed about my mother, for her secret sin was never disclosed. I felt sorry for her; she had to carry that burden alone and pretend in front of us that she was normal.

I did not know what a virgin was, and I did not know what the sin they were referring to so much was either. But whatever it was, they were sure it was filthy and disgusting.

The nuns would actually squint their eyes when they said the word sex or mentioned its filthiness. I can remember one day asking a nun what sex was and why it was so filthy—the suspense was killing me. I should have known better than to ask the question. All the warning signs were there; I knew better. I received a slap on my face that left a handprint for about three days. I never asked that question again.

Sister Paul prepped the class constantly for what was to come in second grade. It was, as she put it, the "The proudest day of your lives."

This proud day of course, was the day we would receive our first Holy Communion. Holy Communion was a small, round piece of flat bread, sort of like a hard, edible piece of cardboard. It was the size of a silver dollar, and the receiver was not given a choice of colors. It was only available in brilliant white, which I thought was lacking in artistic imagination.

The Early Catholic Years

The nuns would constantly explain to the class that the Communion wafer was the body of Christ. They would say it represented his body and that wine represented his blood. It was also known as the "host." During mass the receiver would walk up to the altar, and the priest would have him stick out his tongue, and he would put the Communion on the receivers tongue. We were told that the Communion host was the most sacred thing on earth and that we dare not touch it. That is why only a sacred priest could touch it, because a priest was the closest person on earth to God. Those immortal words were constantly pounded into our minds throughout our eight years at St. John's school:

"A priest is the closest person on earth to God."

There were rumors flying around the classroom at the time, and some of them were scary. I heard from kids in the know that apparently if you got curious and decided to touch the Communion with your fingers while it was in your mouth, your fingers would burn and fall off. You were only allowed to touch it with your tongue. I bought the stories and was determined that there was no way on earth I would ever touch the communion with any unworthy part of me.

The nuns explained that the Communion would dissolve in your mouth, and this left me perplexed. What if my tongue was dirty? Would God know?

And I also could not help but wonder: how could the Communion be pure white, when it was a piece of God's body? I thought it should be red, or look like a piece of steak or something resembling a body part. And was it a part of skin, or was it part of an internal organ? Also, when was the church going to run out of

A Witch Wins JUSTICE

Communion—there are only so many body parts to go around.

In addition, if Communion was really like bread, which the nuns added to the confusion, I envisioned God to be sort of like the Pillsbury Doughboy, with pure white skin and no blood. Maybe, I thought, when he was crucified and bled to death, he ran out of blood, and that was why his body was so white? But how did he turn into bread? Too much information, too many questions, and no satisfactory answers.

Shortly before my first Communion, I was in the church at a practice, and I could not help but stare at the giant crucifix of Jesus on the wall of the church. Given the history the nuns had taught me, I could not make sense out of any of it. Why did he die? Why were we eating some kind of bread and pretending it was pieces of his body? Why was he hanging there for everybody to gaze at, and why on earth would the priest want to drink his blood, or anybody's blood for that matter?

It hit me then, that there was a movie on TV about Dracula, a vampire who drank blood. Did this mean that Catholics were vampires? Was Dracula a priest? I was lost, but none of my classmates seemed to be thinking ahead like I was. I felt confused and lonely.

A very short flashback shot through my mind at that second, and I thought I saw someone on a cross burning to death a long time ago, but where was that? Why did I think that? It frightened me. I left the church as fast as I could, and I did not want to receive the Communion, because it gave me the creeps. I didn't know how to tell Sister Paul. Somehow I got up the courage on the way back to the classroom, and I walked up to her to ask the question.

The Early Catholic Years

As I approached her, I could feel my voice quiver.

"Sister Paul," I shook, "did they burn Jesus after he was crucified?"

The nun looked at me perplexed.

"Why would you ask that?"

"I don't know," I answered with embarrassment. "Didn't they burn people on crosses?"

"Who told you that?" She said harshly.

I had no intention of telling her about my dreams. I was so sorry I had asked her the question.

"I don't know," I managed to squeak out.

Sister Paul was visibly angry and also very curious. I thought the best way out was to act stupid and change the subject. So I did both.

"How come nuns can't touch the Communion, and only priests can?" I said, hoping to erase the issue of the burning cross from her mind. But this got her more pissed off than the other questions.

"Because God only wants priests to touch it, that's why!" she screamed.

She then pulled my ear so hard I thought it was going to come off of my head.

"You should never question what God wants!" she continued. "Now get to the classroom right now."

The pain I felt on my ear was killing me. Thank God I didn't ask her if priests were vampires.

The next day we returned to the church for practice again, and I was scared of the Cross, and of the altar. I was much too close to it. But the altar was a clean scene. There were no signs of blood or fire, and it was draped in a large white cloth, which was not intimidating. There was a chalice on the altar, and I did not want to see the

A Witch Wins JUSTICE

blood inside of it. The nun told us the altar was a very sacred place, and off-limits to us at most times. I was fine with that. And there was no sign of Dracula.

I was afraid to get too close to the altar, being born a rotten sinner, and I had reservations about the whole death scene anyway. I had a secret to hide, and I did not want to share my childhood memories about my dreams of fires or tortures from the past with anyone, for any reason. I was sure God would be cool with that, because He probably knew about them anyway.

Back at home, my mother used to make an altar every year herself in the corner of our living room, and it was an altar she said she made to Mary the Mother of God, instead of making an altar to Jesus. That was fine with me too. One day she told me it was like Grandma's altar, only Grandma had said that Mary was "Diana," and they were much the same. She said that in Naples, the family made altars for Diana, and they were beautiful.

My mother did not say who Diana was, or why her mother called her icon Diana. I did not know for years who Diana was. I assumed it was Mary's other name, or middle name, or something to do with religion. The altar my mother made had candles, flowers, and decorations on it, and looked nothing like the altar in church. It looked more like an altar of comfort, with lots of color.

It was not until several years later that I read books and articles about Diana, the Queen of Witches in Italy. Diana was also worshiped as a goddess in other cultures and Pagan beliefs in other parts of the world, and the name was synonymous with goddess worship and Witchcraft practice in several countries for centuries. My mother never mentioned any of that. What she passed

The Early Catholic Years

on to me was a confusing mixed blend of superstition, Catholicism, and blurry memories of an old belief system she knew very little about.

Her family celebrated *Befana*, which is an ancient Italian Witch folklore tradition, celebrated like Christmas. They made altars to Diana, put salt and figs on the altar, and recited invocations they could not explain. It was obvious to me that she had some kind of mixed traditions passed on to her from Italy, but she was unsure of the meaning and significance, and she certainly was not the exemplary teacher I would have hoped for to teach me the Craft.

Being an Italian Catholic was confusing at home, but being a Catholic at school was much more confusing. Second grade was more of a repeat of first grade, with the exception of the soon to be "proudest day of my life." I was now heavily into the whole Catholic scene. I felt special and pure and righteous, knowing that the day was coming and that I was ready and able to be a worthy receiver. But there was still another bridge to be crossed before the actual day would come.

Wouldn't you know it. Those Catholic ancestors thought of everything. Before you become worthy of receiving God in your mouth and swallowing his flesh, you have to have a clean slate. This involved a cleansing process called "the Sacrament of Confession."

The purpose of confession, we were informed, was to attempt to remove some of the blackness from our inner soul, so that we may be worthy of having the divine priest place the Communion on our tongue. A nun who taught us second grade explained to us in detail how the priests were so pure that only they were able to hear

A Witch Wins JUSTICE

our confessions. Catholic priests, being the holy divine messengers of God himself, were actually capable of removing some of the contaminated filth from our tarnished souls.

"The soul of a priest," she explained with pride, "is by far the most spotless pure white soul that God has created in any man on earth."

"Fortunately for us," she continued, "the holy Catholic priests, unlike any other clergy from any other religion, are the only true, undisputed representatives of almighty God himself here on earth, and the other bogus religions are not capable of this miraculous feat."

I understood that in an attempt to save us from eternal damnation, these spotless priests were willing to stick their necks out and try to cleanse some of the evil sinfulness from our blemished souls, which although no easy task, was a miracle in itself.

Now the rules of this sacrament were to be adhered to very specifically for the sinful contamination to be expunged properly. The sinner would go into a dark room about the size of a telephone booth and kneel on a small wooden bench, and his or her face would be next to a small, screened window. On the other side of the sinner's booth window screen was another booth containing a priest, who sat on his bench. The sinner would kneel down on his or her bench and open the dialogue by saying, "Bless me father for I have sinned, and this is my confession."

The sinner, then, starting at age seven, was supposed to tell the priest all the bad shit he or she has done, all the perverted thoughts and deeds, and all the reasons the sinner was a good candidate for going to hell.

The Early Catholic Years

But at my first confession, I was seven. Not only was I sexless and naïve, I couldn't think of anything juicy at all to tell the priest.

Absolutely nothing.

So that is basically what I said. I knew I would disappoint him.

"Father," I spoke, "I don't have any sins to tell you about."

"What do you mean," he answered. "We all have sins to confess."

So I had to think hard. It was a dilemma. I wasn't going to get out of the little oak-paneled claustrophobic room without some sins spilling out.

"Well I hit my brother, but he hit me first."

It was all I could come up with. I felt an incredible burden lifted from my shoulders.

Then the priest dished out the "penance." Penance is the dues you pay for sinning. It usually consisted of having to say prayers like three "Hail Marys," or two "Our Fathers," or in serious cases, the "Rosary," which was a mammoth cocktail of countless repetitious prayers back-to-back until you either fell asleep or lost your voice.

After the priest gave you your penance, you would proceed to the kneeling bench at the front of the altar pews, in front of all the other students, and say your penance to yourself while looking toward the altar. The other students could calculate by the time you spent at the kneeling bench approximately how long you were praying the penance, and it would indicate how sinful you were by how long you took. It was a flaw in the system, I thought, or it was a clever way for the nuns to figure out how evil you had been.

A Witch Wins JUSTICE

I will never forget the smell of the confessional box at St. John's church. The confessional room was made of wood and had the distinctive smell of old oak paneling, and perhaps some wood polish of some kind. But there was another distinctive smell, one I had smelled before but could not recognize immediately. I later identified the smell as that of alcohol.

For several years, when the priest would talk to me in the confessional, there was a distinct smell of alcohol, and I had associated it with the natural smell of the wood enclosure. I had assumed that the old wood confessional smelled like alcohol because of its age. At that time, I did not realize that the additional smell emanating from the confessional was coming from the priest. I still imagined it was associated with wood or wood polish. I finally became aware of the alcohol being the cause of the smell of the confessional, at a holiday party at my aunt's house two years later, when my Uncle gave me a hug. As his face pressed against mine, I recognized the smell. I will never forget the look on my relatives' faces that day.

"Wow," I said, when Uncle Frank breathed on me.

"You smell just like the wood in the confessional!"

My aunt and mother, who were standing next to me, nearly fainted. This revelation led me years later to ponder whether or not hearing confessions led the priest to drink out of frustration and anxiety, or if the priest drank "for some other reason."

The two priests I knew at the time to be at St. John's church were Fr. Mc Gullicut and Fr. Tollner. Fr. Mc Gullicut was the Pastor, whom I figured at the time to be about 165 years old. He was the head pastor, had gray hair

The Early Catholic Years

and a raisin-wrinkled face, and he resembled "Father Time" from the New Years posters.

Fr. Tollner was much younger and resembled Richard Chamberlain to me. I often heard it said at the time that Fr. Tollner was "just too nice," and was "very handsome." He was so nice, in fact, that he possessed an incredible gift to befriend an astounding number of people, especially female parishioners with young boys. My Aunt Fran was one of those parishioners who was very close to Fr. Tollner.

I became an altar boy a few years later at St. John's, and it was for the most part uneventful, and I managed to cruise through this phase of Catholicism intact, with the exception of witnessing some pretty hardcore drinking in the priests' quarters. A few of the priests felt the need to "taste" the wine in considerable amounts before the mass sometimes.

In the year 1969, the "psychedelic age," when flower power and the hippie age of love was occurring, I was still an altar boy. One priest in particular was extremely disgusted with the way girls would dress up and go to church. Mini skirts had become popular, and many girls would wear them to church. The priest would down a whole bottle of wine in the sacristy, which was the priests' private room behind the altar, and then go on a rant about how filthy the young girls were. He would complain about their short, nasty mini skirts, exposing their flesh for all to see and taunting innocent men with lust and sinful desire, and how naughty and despicable the display of utter filthy sex was. He put the nuns to shame with his take on morals and sexuality.

He would go on to say that the young girls intentionally showed their legs and flesh to enjoy the temptation,

A Witch Wins JUSTICE

to lure otherwise innocent males into the corruption of their souls. His face would turn red, and he would drool like a hungry, mad animal. Then he would go out of the sacristy in this condition, to the altar to say mass, and stare at all the sinful dirty girls, and their filthy display of vulgar exhibitionism.

And he would stare, and stare, and stare.

It seemed to me that he was in anguish and that he was on the verge of some kind of heart failure brought on by the witnessing of something so evil and dangerous—that his heart was going to go into arrest at any second.

What a lesson that was.

Sinful, vulgar, filthy, dirty, naughty, lustful, sexual flesh. I heard these words over and over again. In all different combinations, on several Sundays.

But his contempt for women as sexual beings, and his negative reactions, seemed abnormal to me in a way that I could not process. One time in particular, he referred to the girls wearing the lustful miniskirts as "Witches."

I felt myself wander off as he said this; his anger and hatred when using the word "Witch" sent me mentally off into space. I didn't know why, but I was lost as he ranted this time, and I felt as though I was in a different building, like in my nightmares years before, and when I looked at him he had no face. I did a double take and popped back into awareness, wondering why I had this reaction.

I was surprised at the time he mentioned witches, but later on in my life as I recalled his words, the meaning became much more alarming to me. It represented to me the disturbed mind of the witch hunters and torturers in Catholic history who condemned innocent women and young girls as witches, hating them for their sexuality and actually killing them for it, because of the guilt and confusion in their own twisted heads.

It was frightening to watch this priest both drool over and hate the girls at the same instant, because I could not understand how the two feelings could merge together, and I did not want him to share his sickness with me. I wanted so badly to get away from this scene at the time, and I felt a familiar creepiness about it, but I was still unable to identify the source of it. It seemed unnatural and irrational, yet it was taking place in the house of God.

I watched this same priest one Sunday peering through the doorway, staring intently at two girls in skirts sitting in the pew, and I watched him sweating and wiping his brow, his face beet red, mumbling about how short their skirts were, and how much it hurt him to see it all. He jumped when he turned and saw me looking at him, and he snarled at me angrily, his fists clenched in rage.

"For God's sake lad," he belted, "now go get me a damp towel to wipe my face!"

Thank God there was so much wine available in the rectory. Perhaps it was the best way to wipe the memory of the filthy miniskirted girls from his mind. Then, there was Fr. Tollner. He didn't seem to notice the nasty girls wearing the filthy mini skirts at all. Fr. Tollner could walk by the filthiest, shortest, nastiest miniskirts in the entire parish completely undaunted. I thought at the time that he must have been a tower of religious strength and

A Witch Wins JUSTICE

high moral character, impervious to any temptation displayed whatsoever.

Fr. Tollner came to my Aunt Fran's house for dinners, birthdays, and holidays for years. All of my relatives knew him. He was especially fond of my cousin Curt, who was about five years older than I was. My cousin Curt and other young boys would go places with Fr. Tollner on occasions, because Fr. Tollner was "so with the times."

When I was in sixth grade, about the age of eleven, I rode my bicycle to my Aunt Fran's house to pull weeds for money on a Saturday. She had left her key in her mailbox for me, and I arrived at her house in the afternoon. Aunt Fran and her family were in Lake Tahoe, she had told me, and I was to do some garden work, and she had said that I could go into the house for soda if I wanted to.

I took the key and opened the door, and went into the kitchen to get a soda.

I then heard noises in one of the bedrooms down the hall, and was startled because I thought that the house was empty. Then I heard footsteps in the hall, and a bedroom door shut. I had visions of a burglar coming out of the room to attack me next, but instead my cousin Curt walked out of the room.

"Joey," he said, "what are you doing here?"

"I came to pull the weeds and do the garden," I answered.

Curt looked shaken. Behind him, I caught a glimpse of a tall dark figure, who was trying to slip by as though he were trying to leave without me seeing his face.

It was Fr. Tollner.

The Early Catholic Years

I walked toward Fr. Tollner because I wanted to say hi. It never occurred to me to question why he was there.

"Hi Fr. Tollner," I blurted excitedly.

But the priest looked distraught, which eluded me at the time. He continued to walk toward the front door as though I wasn't there. Puzzled, I walked toward him in the hallway. It was then for the first time in my life I smelled marijuana, and I did not know it. Curt must had seen me sniffing the air, and he said lowly, before I could ask, "I was burning incense."

"It smells good," I said.

Tollner smiled a weak grin and mumbled something about how he must be going. I never put two and two together until years later. Fr. Tollner was in my teenage cousin's bedroom, alone with him. The door was shut, Curt's parents were out of town, and they were smoking pot.

There was another incident when I was twelve. We were at a holiday function at my Aunt Fran's house, and Fr. Tollner was there as usual. It was late, and the adults at the party were drinking and dancing, having a great festive time like Italians do at those things. Fr. Tollner was standing near me talking to someone, and he overheard one of my uncles ask me if I wanted something to drink.

Trying to be a clown, I said, "I'll have a beer."

My uncle laughed and slapped the top of my head and walked away.

Tollner looked at me, and with a devious smile whispered,

"Do you really want a beer?"

Not knowing if he was serious, I pretended to laugh and then walked away, wondering what had just

A Witch Wins JUSTICE

happened. I went into my cousin Curt's room, looking at the posters on his walls, and Tollner followed me into the room. No one else was there, and Tollner shut the door and handed me a beer. I thought it might have been a trick, or perhaps a test of some sort.

"Shh," he smiled. "This is our little secret."

I was surprised and slowly took the beer from his hand, and he didn't stop me. I took a sip. He sipped his own drink and looked at me approvingly.

"Ah" he started, "you're old enough to have one beer anyway."

"Yeah," I responded, hiding my shock, "sure I am."

"Did you just get new pants?" he asked, looking at my new corduroy pants that I was so proud of.

"Yeah, I did," I beamed.

"They're cool," he said. "They sure fit you nice." "They're nice and tight."

"Thanks," I answered.

But I felt a little awkward. I didn't know exactly why, but the conversation seemed a bit strange. Tollner winked at me then left the room. I hid the beer, thinking that Fr. Tollner was the coolest priest on earth and that I was very special. Little did I know at the time that Fr. Tollner would turn out to be the worst child sexual offender to have ever been at St. John's school and would later be literally caught in the act of child molestation, with multiple lawsuits and claims filed against him. I had escaped being molested that night, probably because the house was full of people and Fr. Tollner, beloved priest to my Aunt Fran, did not have enough time to abuse me.

Years later, when my cousin Curt was thirty-three, I went to visit him in the hospital, and he was lying there

The Early Catholic Years

motionless, his eyes closed, dying of AIDS. As I sat there next to his bed on his last day in the ICU, all I could think about was Fr. Tollner grooming him, what I had walked in on years before, and how stupid I had felt about myself. I closed my eyes while I sat in the room.

When I opened them seconds later, I was eleven, and the sweet smell of marijuana had filled the hospital room, and Curt opened his eyes and smiled at me.

"Don't worry Joey, it's only incense, and Fr. Tollner is just visiting. I'm going to sleep now. You're just a little boy; you would never understand."

"I know," I answered. "It is only incense. I won't say a word. And I thought Fr. Tollner was just visiting you too."

Then Curt laughed weakly in the smoky marijuana-filled hospital room, and went quietly to sleep for the last time.

I was growing tired of Catholic mass and church, partially because I felt it was boring, and partially because I was getting nothing spiritual from it.

The weirdness I noticed about the priests was accumulating, but I still regarded them as being the closest people to God, probably as a result of the repetitious teachings I'd had as a child, and not because they had displayed anything to me that suggested they were spiritual human beings. I sensed some sort of conflict.

What bothered me most was the interpretation of women as sinful by some of the priests; it seemed distorted, and I still couldn't process their views and actions when others were not around. I felt as though I needed something else, although I did not know what it was or how to find it. The only thing I really liked about going to

A Witch Wins JUSTICE

church, honestly, was looking at the girls in their miniskirts, even if they were "filthy and nasty."

I did not share the disturbed views of some of the priests about the girls. I thought the girls were attractive, beautiful, and awesome. Nature, I felt, did a wonderful job of designing them. But I would never tell a holy priest my views on the subject; I avoided the discussion entirely.

As I turned thirteen, I was happy I was finally going to leave St. John's, graduate, and become "me." I wondered who I was and what I had become, and I did not question why I was here. Life was unexplained at this point, yet still so acceptable at the same time. My future was ahead of me—this I knew, and I knew that it would only get better. So far I was capable of getting "A"s in school with little effort, and I felt as though I could easily take on high school like anybody else, and possibly better with a bit more effort.

I had been told that I scored high on IQ tests given all through grade school, although what an IQ was did not concern me in my first eight years of grammar school.

Throughout my childhood, and all through grammar school, I went to church every Sunday with my mother, father, brothers, and sisters. I had grown accustomed to being a practicing Catholic, and it was assumed to be the way life would always be. We lived in a three-bedroom two-bath house, and at the age of twelve I asked my parents if I could convert our one-car garage into my own bedroom. They were surprised, but they said yes. So I put up a wall to divide the room in two, and the wall separated the laundry room off of the hallway leading

The Early Catholic Years

into the garage, and my new bedroom became the rest of the garage. I installed a short doorway and door into my new room.

It was at that time that I realized I could use hammers, saws, and building tools, and I did not know where the knowledge and skills came from, but it came to me very easily. My father did not train me or even help me; he was not in the building trades at all. After I completed the room it occurred to me that perhaps I had incarnated skills that were induced instinctively, which is not a Catholic belief. Later on in life, the building skills would prove to be an asset.

Since it was 1969, the height of the psychedelic age, I was very into the new colorful arts of the time. Almost every day, I would paint a small picture on my new bedroom wall with different latex paints. The pictures would all mesh and blend with each other like a collage, and by the end of the year, the entire twelve-foot wall on one side of the bedroom was completely covered with hundreds of pictures, and psychedelic images and words. It was a giant mural, hand-painted and finely detailed. My friends were very impressed, and my mother would proudly show the mural to any company or relatives who would visit. I gained a reputation in my circle of Italian relatives as the "artist of the family." Again, I had no idea where this skill originated; I had no training in any art classes.

I was convinced that I was a normal teenager but skinny, short, and small for my age—a drawback, though I somewhat managed to persuade most others my age that I was more confidant than I truly was, which may have been typical. Girls interested me for sure, but I must

A Witch Wins JUSTICE

admit I was afraid of them. They seemed more mature than the boys, smarter on the whole, and definitely more attractive. They seemed magnetic in a mysterious sort of way, and they had the ability to make me nervous inside, and I was determined to hide it to the point that I was not able to think clearly when talking to them, because I was concentrating so much on not looking or sounding as though I was stupid.

The psychedelic age presented a new era of social structures and divisions, and new adventures in culture, music, and arts. There were bell-bottoms, flowers, peace signs, and talk of drugs that I had never heard of before, and public interest in witchcraft and magick was on the rise. I was bombarded with a lot of information toward the end of eighth grade.

Finally the long anticipated Salesian High School exam was scheduled.

No problem. A ten-second prayer to Jesus the night before, and it was a slam-dunk. Jesus and I were still very tight.

It was also in 1969 that I began to appreciate my own choice of music, mostly rock and pop, and Jimi Hendrix was at his best. I also liked a song produced by a local band about a young girl and the city of Mendocino, which was about the fantasy love of my life. She was a "teenybopper" I'd never met, in a city I'd never been to, in a life I'd never known. But the song was relevant to me for some reason; it was a representation of whom I thought I could be like, because I believed I had not really established my own identity yet. It was also relevant because it incited feelings of a future of adventure and excitement.

The Early Catholic Years

Something to dream positively about. To wonder about.

Looking back, I realize that the real beauty of youth was looking forward to what I thought the world would be like for me, because I had not experienced it yet. The innocent anticipation of an exhilarating life that awaited me was like the preparation for a vacation, full of wonder and excitement, before the trip takes place. I had not been disappointed yet with a bad outcome, and the whole world seemed like it had so much to offer, like in a lot of the songs that I just knew were written for me ahead of my time. Anticipation for the sake of itself was so rewarding. So clean. So enticing.

And then there was sex. The mystery word, from an unknown mystery world. We couldn't say it loudly at Catholic school—partly because Jesus may be listening, and partly because the nuns may be listening, and partly because we did not know what it really was. But we acted like we knew all about it. To be honest, I didn't have a clue. Some of the theories presented by some of the guys on the playground didn't seem quite right, and I was a little confused. More like scared. I can't rationalize here; I was a late bloomer. Some of the guys in my class were talking about shaving, and I felt like I was thirteen years old going on ten. I learned bits and pieces about sex through the years in grammar school from some of the older boys, whose descriptions, stories, half-truths, and bragging did not match the descriptions or feelings presented by the mostly silent nuns. And the drunken priests' twisted views on the filthiness of flesh and female lust was out of the question.

A Witch Wins JUSTICE

To make matters more complicated for me, a new concept found its way into the school hall whispers that year and was totally unexpected. It was concerning the new words and terms introduced by the loudmouth, obnoxious schoolyard bullies: the colorful terms "fag," "queer," "fruit," and "homo."

Up until that year, I had never heard those terms before, but I quickly learned that the words referred to "boys who like boys."

Now this was really perplexing. It had never occurred to me at all that a boy could "like" a boy. As a matter of fact, I didn't believe that the possibility could exist. It took some convincing by some of the guys at school that it did really happen and that there were witnesses who had actually seen such things. Shortly thereafter, most of the boys began calling each other any and all combinations of these terms, and this continued well into high school.

The summer after eighth grade when I was thirteen was the very last normal Catholic summer I would ever have. I didn't know it at the time. I went almost daily that summer to the Catholic Church swim center, and on the last day of summer, I broke my arm at the swimming pool. So I would be entering ninth grade with a cast on my left arm.

There's a lot that goes on in a boy's head when he is thirteen and he thinks he's miles behind his peers in the "male" department. I could talk then about music, cars, and a limited amount of sports, but the sex scene for me was nonexistent.

"Just wait till I'm fourteen," I thought.

God is a concept...by which we measure our pain.

—JOHN LENNON

Into the Salesian High School of Horrors

My introduction into high school wasn't bad. Somewhere along the line I was told I was to enter the homeroom class of the higher achievers on the entrance exam. I think I had expected it, but I was not exactly sure, because I did not know how many people had actually taken the exam test, nor from where they had come. The nuns at St John's Elementary had prepped us that it was a very high honor to be accepted into the famous Salesian High School at all.

Salesian High was a small Catholic campus compared to neighboring public schools at the time. The total student school population for grades nine through twelve was less than four hundred students. We were told it was because most entrance exam takers couldn't cut the mustard. Imagine my pride. I weighed in at about eighty-five pounds when I was thirteen, and I think my head weighed eighty pounds. That pride lasted about two minutes after I entered the school grounds. It was overshadowed, literally, by the hundred-sixty-pound poster-boy hulks that shook the ground walking past me on admission day.

A Witch Wins JUSTICE

Salesian was an all-male Catholic School, and the teachers and staff were predominantly priests and "brothers." The priests, of course, were the respected flawless creatures whom I still considered the closest thing on earth to God. The brothers were, as I thought, men who were practicing and studying to be priests but weren't "ordained" yet, which is like graduating to be a priest. But they were still to be respected, because they were on their way. There were some "laymen" teachers, who were regular men that were not "of the cloth" so to speak.

The Salesian Order of Catholic priests was created because of the "work" performed over a hundred years ago by a man named Don Bosco, or John Bosco. This man, we were told, took in and cared for young boys that were orphans or had troubles. He loved young boys and was very holy. The Salesian priests followed the example of the "Saint Don Bosco" by also helping many young boys. This should have been some sort of "Red Flag" to some adults somewhere, but boys beginning high school were still very naïve at the time.

But the introduction to Salesian got weird fast. The school had a traditional "freshman initiation day," which was, in my eyes, pretty disgusting. Every year, apparently, the seniors in the school would dig a large trench and fill it with mud, water, and garbage, and the incoming freshman would have to "swim" through the wet debris. The purpose of this ritual was to "initiate" the freshmen by flagrant humiliation. How Catholic is that?

I went to see the preparation for this "initiation," and I was floored. I saw seniors pouring the expected usual garbage into the ditch and into the muddy water

Into the Salesian High School of Horrors

solution, but there was more. I actually witnessed seniors peeing in the muddy solution, shoveling dog crap into the solution and various chemicals from the "lab." It was at that point I decided not to partake in the freshmen initiation swim. When the freshmen got into their gym shorts and were sent into the muck, I refused. I used the little cast on my broken wrist as an excuse. I didn't care if they called me a wimp. There was just no way I was going to partake in the initiation swim from hell.

My brother Anthony was a year older than I, and he had obviously been sent to Salesian before I had. He was a clown. More into sports than I, and more into "goofing off." We took the bus to school, and sometimes we got a ride from mom or dad. My mother started to work at the school cafeteria about the same time I started Salesian, and then we would all ride together in the mornings on most days. Our family was not well-off financially, but this never seemed to be an issue.

At the west side of the school, across the field, was the Salesian Boys Club. It had Ping-Pong, pool tables, and a small indoor basketball court. "Brother Sal Billante" ran the Boys Club. Brother Sal had short hair, usually wore shorts and sneakers, and occasionally had a camera with him. My brother would go there after school sometimes to play basketball, and I would go to play pool. It wasn't long after I began my first year at Salesian that I noticed that Fr. Steve Whelan would also go to the Boys Club.

Fr. Steve Whelan was the vice principal of the school. He was a tall, medium-built man, probably in his thirties, with receding hairline and long black sideburns. He had "buck" teeth, as we called them, and the students referred to him as "the gopher." He was very unattractive, I thought, and seemed strange in a way I could neither explain nor analyze. "Creepy" comes to mind. Sometimes I would think I saw Fr. Whelan watching me, and I would turn around, and he would be staring intently at me. It was uncomfortable, and I was unsure what was going on. Then he would smile at me, and I would dismiss it as though it was nothing.

Fr. Whelan approached me one day, early in my 1969 freshman year, to talk about "spirit ribbons." These were colorful school ribbons about an inch wide by five inches long, he explained, that were to be sold for supporting the different sports games at the school. They had slogans on them for different games, which said things like "Beat the Panthers," and so on. Why he chose me to sell them, I did not know, at least at that time. Whelan also chose one other boy that I was aware of at the time, to sell the spirit ribbons. His name was Steve Brom, and he was one year ahead of me at Salesian.

After school one day early in my freshman year, I went to the Boys Club to play pool, and I was by myself. As I started to walk across the field toward the Boys Club, all of a sudden Fr. Whelan was beside me. I am sure he had been watching me, and he joined me as though we were best friends. He put his arm on my shoulder, and smiled excitedly.

"Where are you going?" he asked.

"To play pool at the Boys Club," I said.

"Well, can I join you?" he popped.

"I don't care," I said.

But I did. I felt weird. It felt awkward. Why in the world would he want to join me at pool? I wasn't any good. It didn't click. But a short while later I was to find out. We walked into the Boys Club; I grabbed a cue stick, and so did Fr. Whelan.

"You break," he said.

"Okay," I answered.

Then I broke the first rack. I shot again, and then I missed.

"You go," I said.

But Whelan just sat there on the bench, which was behind the pool table against a wall. He was wearing a long black priest robe, which came all the way down to his ankles. I turned to look at him, and I almost fainted. He was sitting about four feet away from me, slouched down on the bench, and his hands were inside his robe. He was very obviously masturbating, and his robe at his crotch line was jerking up and down. His hands were moving up and down on himself, and it looked as though he was drooling. His eyes were half closed.

In a sandy whispering voice he said,

"You keep playing, I want to watch you."

I felt my eyes open so wide I thought that they would fall out of my head. I turned around and felt a cold sweat on the back of my neck, and I thought I should run. But then, Brother Sal Billante walked by us and looked at Whelan. He looked a little shocked at first, and then he stopped.

"Thank God," I thought.

How embarrassing, but thank God Brother Sal saw this.

But the next shocker was closer than I thought. Brother Sal just stood and watched Whelan and me. He had a wicked smile on his face and seemed to really enjoy this

A Witch Wins JUSTICE

show. By now I could feel sweat dripping down the side of my face, and my face was so hot and red I thought it would burst. My mind was racing for a solution. What the hell is going on? What should I do? I tried to act as though nothing was happening and made a feeble effort to shoot again, but I was shaking so badly. Seconds turned to hours. Then finally Whelan was "finished," and he got up and went to the bathroom to clean up, I guess. I was afraid to watch him. Bro. Sal Billante stayed the whole time. He watched the entire masturbation show.

Setting the cue stick down to regain my wits, I still was a bit frozen. Not to worry though, Bro. Sal Billante walked over to me and put his hand on my butt. He patted it lightly, I imagine for consolation, or maybe for congratulations, or maybe it was some sort of Salesian offering of welcome to the club. Whatever the case, I looked at the cross of Jesus on the wall and wondered if Jesus had turned his head. This was the first time in my life that I was actually pissed off at Jesus.

I saw Brother Sal Billante and Fr. Whelan a few days later, and they were talking on the school grounds. I know they both saw me, and I could sense they were talking about me. Not hearing their conversation, I felt a cold chill when they both looked at me and broke a wide smile. Then they were silent. A chilly, devious silence. They knew that I suspected something, but I wasn't clear what that something was.

No longer than a few days later, I went back to the Boys Club to play pool again, and Fr. Whelan wasn't there. Maybe it was his day off of masturbation duty; I didn't know. But Billante was there. He came over to me and gave me the usual friendly Salesian pat on the ass, then went over to the basketball court. To my surprise and apparent ignorance, I saw Billante pat all the boys on the butt. Maybe this was a sports thing, I thought. None of the boys reacted to it, as though they were all used to it. This made me feel more comfortable, thinking that it's just a manly "pat your player's butt" thing, it's cool. But that short-lived theory was blown out of the water when an older student walked up to me to join me in a game of pool.

He looked in the direction of where Billante was and said to me, "Don't you think it's kinda queer that Bro. Sal always pats everybody's ass all day long?" "I think he's probably a fag."

Fag was the wrong word.

His take on Bro. Sal being strange was accurate. Bro. Sal Billante was convicted years later for multiple counts of child molestation and lewd acts of sexual abuse. Billante spent several years in San Quentin prison. "Queer" and "fag" were the wrong words. "Child abuser" was the correct term, but the student who said that was referring to Billante's need to touch the boys, which was right on track. The red flag should have been up in my mind then, because Billante and Whelan were so close, and I should have sensed their unusual closeness around the Boys Club. But I was still an eighty-five-pound square peg, at the wrong time and at the wrong place. I could still pass for ten most anywhere I went. I think Fr. Whelan must have noticed that trait and liked the fact that I looked much younger than I was.

Shortly after, I became aware that Whelan was "watching me." More like stalking me. I would see him in the hallways, near the bathrooms, and at lunchtime

A Witch Wins JUSTICE

and PE time, staring at me. Not being gifted at deduction at this age, I sort of shrugged it off. But little by little, it would become more obvious. So obvious in fact, that other kids started to notice. It didn't seem to become a serious problem until Whelan started to come into the boys' showers at the end of PE classes. And his Boys Club "activities" increased.

My next bad experience at the Boys Club wasn't long after. I went to play pool, as usual, and Whelan wasn't around. At least I thought he wasn't. He must have had a "matter-transfer" unit like on Star Trek, because I took a shot at a pool ball and then turned around, and he was already sitting there again masturbating before I could blink. I was alone, and I stood frozen there for a minute, unable to think clearly about what to do again.

"Keep playing," he said. "I like to watch you."

Déjà vu. I've been here before, and I've heard that before. Now what?

Just about then, a classmate of mine, Johnny, walked into the Boys Club, and headed right towards me. I was grateful. Hoping he would see what was going on, I looked toward Whelan, thinking Whelan would get embarrassed and cut his act short. But Whelan continued. Maybe he didn't see Johnny walk up to me.

"Can I play pool with you?" Johnny asked.

"Sure." I answered dumbfounded, wondering why Johnny did not see Whelan.

I decided to point it out. I walked quietly up toward Johnny and whispered.

"Look at Fr. Steve."

Johnny looked at Fr. Steve and did a double take.

"He's got a huge boner!" he laughed out loud.

Into the Salesian High School of Horrors

Johnny's reaction took me by surprise; I had expected him to be as repulsed as I was. He just kept laughing.

"Does he always do that?" he asked.

"I've seen him do that more than once," I answered disappointingly.

But it did not seem to faze Johnny the way it fazed me. Perhaps it was a shock-induced reaction, I don't know. To make matters worse, Bro. Sal was watching again. This was too much for me. Johnny made a remark about Fr. Steve "jerking off," and he left. I looked up at the cross on the wall, and I was sure Jesus was turning his head away again. I may have called Jesus an idiot for being so cavalier about it.

Maybe everybody was getting used to this, or maybe Johnny was insensitive to it for some reason, but I was disturbed. Very disturbed. I do know now that Johnny was expelled from the Salesian school not long after the incident, but I never discussed it anymore at the school with him. What I thought would be my saving moment for validation, proved to be a let down. I was on my own again.

As bad stories have a way of continuing, this one did. Perhaps it was Bro. Sal Billante's debased approval that encouraged Whelan, or my bad fate. Maybe it was a combination of the two, who knows. But the stalking and staring at all different times by Whelan escalated. I noticed more and more that he was trying to follow me to catch me in the bathroom. The Salesian school bathrooms had no doors at the entrances; perhaps this was the idea of a voyeuristic clergyman in the past. I could see Whelan watching me at the urinals, where the boys would stand to do their business. His spying was

A Witch Wins JUSTICE

comparable to that of a sick peeping tom one would see frequenting old bowling alley restrooms.

But worse than that, Whelan would come into the boys' locker/shower room after PE to watch me strip, to get in the shower naked. Not that he didn't watch other boys, but he *really* watched me. What added to my frustration was that Whelan was not our PE instructor and had no "business" in the shower room after PE. I knew he was there for me. He watched me strip with a perverse intense glare that made me cringe. This happened much too often. Every once in a while, I would hear someone comment about the situation, but no one did anything to stop it.

"Don't you think it's weird that Fr. Steve comes into the shower room so much?" "He doesn't even teach a PE class."

Mr. Shaugnessy, the PE teacher, who was a layman, did nothing about Whelan's presence, which was very disappointing. I always wondered why.

As Whelan's presence increased in the shower room, I was getting desperate for some kind of help, but was afraid to ask for it. I felt I had no one to confide in or to tell what I really felt was going on. I felt alone. I think Whelan knew this.

He was watching me one day after the PE class came into the shower room, and I was trying to change by my locker. I was cowering down, trying to hide behind my clothes, and he approached me. I was horrified.

"Are you clean?" he asked with a snarl.

I couldn't speak. I was shaking, and he was enjoying it. That was the final straw. So I made a plan. I was so desperate after that, I would go up to the water faucet

Into the Salesian High School of Horrors

after PE class and get a huge gulp of water in my mouth. Then, I would pull my shirt up over my head, and while my shirt was up over my head hiding my face, I would spit the water into my hands, while no one could see, and then put the water into my hair, so that my hair would look wet.

Then, instead of stripping and going into the shower, I would put my clothes on. Since my hair was wet, I fooled my PE coach, Mr. Shaughnessy, into thinking I had taken a shower when he made the last-minute rounds to see if everybody had showered. I did this so many times that it became obvious to the boy whose locker was next to me. His name was Billy. One day, he watched me do it. He knew that I was doing it to avoid the showers. So he spoke up.

"Hey Joe, how come you never take a shower?"

I felt two inches tall. I couldn't answer. I couldn't explain. I felt like I had just been busted for drug possession or robbery, or an unthinkable crime. I just hoped that not too many people had heard him. If they did, I felt that I should just leave the school right then and there and never return.

I noticed toward the end of the term that Steve, the other boy that Whelan had picked to sell the school ribbons, was also dodging Fr. Whelan in the showers, and putting water in his hair outside the locker room, and not taking showers. It was no surprise at that time that the only other boy that Whelan had chose had also done the same thing.

As the locker-room stalking changed the course of my thinking, and perhaps my personality and being, so did the bathroom stalking. It became more evident to me that things were taking a turn for the worse—again. To go to the bathroom, I would go upstairs then down the hall, then downstairs again, all to dodge Whelan and hope that I could get to the bathroom unseen. One unforgettable day, I went through this maze of "ditching the priest" to get to the bathroom, and when I got there—unnoticed, I had hoped– I couldn't urinate.

I stood there at the urinal, and for the first time in my life, I couldn't go, because I was so afraid he was watching. I kept turning around to see if he was there in the doorway, but he was not. I still couldn't go. It was both puzzling and frustrating. I had to wait until I got home several hours later to go urinate in peace and quiet. From that day on, I have not been able to urinate in a public bathroom at the men's urinal. The feeling of being watched by a creep in the bathroom has never left me. I can't accurately count how many times I was stalked in the bathrooms and in the locker room. It was too many, and I have tried to erase them. My guess would be dozens of times. And the long-term effect was forever.

And the rest of my world as I knew it was changing, and it was changing in ways that I didn't always see at first. Like my classes. I found myself doodling and drawing during class and not paying attention. It wasn't unusual for a teen to do this in class, I am aware, but it was unusual for me. Unusual, because I was drawing disgusting pictures that I never drew before, and unusual because I started to hate school. I had never hated school before. And it wasn't because of drugs, drinking, girls on my mind, or any "typical" early teenage distractions. It was because I was beginning to hate the priests, and it was spilling over to the other teachers as well. I felt as though I was miscast and did not belong. I realized that I resented *every* priest and teacher at this point.

I started to become cynical and mistrusting of the entire faculty. I couldn't understand why Whelan had chosen me, and I wondered daily if this kind of thing was happening to anyone else. It would have been a relief if one of my friends had confided to me that they too were being stalked by a priest, but that never happened. Possibly the reason no one confided in me was because they too were silent about their abuse and they were no different than I. I was suspicious that Steve Brom, the other unfortunate Whelan choice, was also enduring the same shadowing by the same predator. Steve Brom later died at an early age, I found out, and I never had the chance to confront him about Whelan.

All year long, I was still selling the "spirit ribbons" to the other students, one for fifteen cents and two for a quarter. Whelan would meet me during lunch, or break, to talk about the money I collected or supposed school issues. But I knew better. He would almost always put his arm around me and pretend to be the caring priest, but I was so uncomfortable. I had the impression he thought we were close because of the masturbation incidents and because I had kept quiet about them.

One day during lunch break, Whelan approached me on the lawn on the west side of the main building, and my friends were about twenty feet away, talking. They were looking toward me, and Whelan came up to me and put his arm around me to talk about "ribbons." I could see my friends looking at me, and they were watching intently and whispering to each other. I could see they thought it was odd. I got away from Whelan

A Witch Wins JUSTICE

as quickly as I was able and walked over to my friends, hoping to convince myself that I was normal, like them.

But one of the boys spoke out.

"Hey Joey, how come you're always with Fr. Steve?" he grinned.

The boys all laughed out loud, and I was embarrassed and speechless.

"Maybe he's his girlfriend," another boy said.

This brought out another wave of laughter.

"No, I think Joey's his Bitch," a third boy answered.

This brought them all to their knees with laughter. It was all I could handle. The humiliation was unbearable, and I felt like a puddle of shit, as they say.

Then I noticed that Fr. Frank Vranjos, a counselor at the school, had been walking by when he heard their jokes and comments. The boys headed off to the cafeteria without me, and Fr. Frank called me over to him.

"Are you alright, Joey?" he asked.

"I guess so," I answered unconvincingly.

"Don't listen to them," he said calmly. "They're just teasing you."

"But I really don't like the way Fr. Steve always touches me," I said. "It bothers me."

"Well, you know, Joey, Fr. Steve is a lot like St. Don Bosco, the founder of the Salesians," he added.

"He likes to be around boys, and he was always close to them, and that's what Salesians is about."

"Well it still bothers me," I answered.

But Fr. Frank wasn't done with his strange consolation. "Well let me tell you a story," he said.

"Did you ever hear the saying, 'any port in a storm'?"

"No," I answered.

Into the Salesian High School of Horrors

"Well, you know, Joey, when sailors are out to sea for a long time," he continued, "and the sea gets rough, and they need to go back home, and they aren't sure if they can make it to the home port, well, they will go to the nearest port. Thus the saying, 'Any port in a storm will do.' Now do you understand?"

He just confused me even more.

"No, I don't understand."

So Fr. Frank continued.

"Okay, say the sailors are out to sea, they haven't seen their wives, or girlfriends, or loved ones for over six months, well, men are only human, they have their weaknesses. So they would seek out the nearest port in the storm. Now do you understand?"

I stared at him in utter confusion.

"No, I don't have any idea what you mean."

Fr. Frank patted me on the back. I imagine he gave up trying to explain whatever it was he was attempting to get across to me.

"It's okay," he said, and then he left me standing there.

I did not realize what he was talking about until about two years later. It was in a "religion" class later on in high school that he told the same exact "Any port in a storm" story to the entire class. Some of the guys in the class smirked and nudged each other.

"Fr. Frank is saying that if women aren't around, and you get horny, then it's okay to have sex with anybody that's there. 'Any port in a storm,' get it?"

How stupid I felt then. Had Fr. Frank actually tried to hint to me that a relationship between a man and a boy was acceptable? Was he trying to rationalize Fr. Steve's

A Witch Wins JUSTICE

behavior? I could have slapped myself. I could have slapped him. But instead, and as usual, I blamed myself for being stupid. I felt as though the IQ I thought that I had which was "above normal" was diminishing as the years went by.

I managed to complete my freshman year with acceptable grades, but Whelan and his perverted antics were taking a toll on me. I was developing a hatred more and more for school, and increasingly more for him.

He happened to meet me on the staircase one day, as I approached the landing.

He appeared out of nowhere. It must have been one of those days he was stalking me and I didn't see him. I turned toward the landing, and all of a sudden he was right in my face.

An inch from my face. And he was so disgusting. I backed away with a wince; I felt physically ill. He was chomping some gum like a horse, with his big horse teeth, and the smell of the gum from that horse face made me want to vomit.

"What are you doing?" I heard myself say out loud.

"I just had some gum, and my breath is kissing sweet," he said as though he were proud.

To my horror, he tried to kiss my mouth. I backed away and almost fell over.

My stomach turned. I could even hear it.

"What is the matter with you?" I yelled. "You're a priest."

To my further horror and complete surprise he said, "Yes but I'm a man too, and men have needs."

That gum.

That horrible gum.

Into the Salesian High School of Horrors

It made me want to throw up. I really wanted to throw up as much as I could. If I could have found out what gum that was, I would have destroyed all of it that I could find in any store.

I had always chewed gum, ever since I could remember, and it had never occurred to me that gum could be so horrible when chewed by perverts "with needs." I was so repulsed, I don't know how I left the scene. But I literally had nightmares about that big ugly face. More like involuntary flashback images, of that big ugly horse face, chomping on that horrible horse gum.

But Fr. "Sweet Breath" wasn't done yet. There was more to come. Now that he knew I was resistant, he became more hostile. I guess that's how these things work. I am sure he liked it better when I was more naive and scared and more quiet. So the abuse began to escalate. I was about fourteen then, but I still looked like I was eleven. Not a great improvement, but I was finally into the ninety-pound range, and I was looking forward to hitting the hundred-pound line soon. Perhaps that's why he chose me.

The goddamn scale was my enemy.

I just couldn't hit that hundred-pound line. I hated that scale. I threw it in the garbage, where it belonged, with horrible horse face gum, never to return. Unfortunately, I couldn't throw away the whole Salesian School. It was still there.

I can't really say how it started a few days later, but for some reason I said or did something in class that made my teacher send me down to the office. Then I was sent to the principal, who in turn sent me to Fr. Whelan's office. The horrible Salesian cycle of terror. Wouldn't you know it.

A Witch Wins JUSTICE

He greeted me with anger, maybe because of the kissing rejection a while back, I don't know. He stood behind his large desk, and told me to sit down.

I did.

Then, for some odd reason, he said he had to leave the room.

"Stay right here, and don't move; I will be right back," he said.

He left the room, and I sat for about five minutes, I don't know exactly, but then he returned. After he walked into the office, he shut the door. The windows of his office and his door had opaque glass that you could not see through. How convenient.

He went behind his desk and opened the drawer. He looked at me with a frown on his scowling face and was abrupt.

"Where is it," he growled.

I looked at him, puzzled.

"Where is what?" I answered.

"Where is it," he yelled louder.

"Where is what?" I answered again.

Then he asked again, the same thing over and over. This scene went on like an idiot contest for several minutes.

Finally he jumped up and said, "Where is the bag of marijuana I had in my desk? I confiscated it from Gary Milsaps. It was here when I left this room, and now it's gone. What did you do with it?"

He seemed convincing, but I didn't know then if I believed him. I had been alone in the room, and no one came in, and I didn't dare go in his desk myself, so I felt it was impossible for a bag of marijuana to disappear by itself. I wouldn't have known if there was a bag of it there anyway. It didn't make sense.

But Whelan continued. "What did you do with it?" he barked.

I know he saw I was mystified. But he was playing out his game.

He came over to me and said something to the effect that he knew I must have it on me. So that was it. He wanted to search me, but he wanted to be rough too.

So Whelan started to grab me to "search" for the dope, which we both knew was not in my possession. He stuck his hands in my pockets, front and back, and had a field day grabbing, pinching, squeezing, fondling, and groping, like a wild deviate. He was trying to hurt me.

That's when I drifted off.

Novocaine. Novocaine.

All I could think of was novocaine.

I don't like going to the dentist.

But there I was. In the dentists office. And I was watching that needle I hate so much. It was full of novocaine. Novocaine hurts so much when the dentist sticks it in your skin, but after about a minute, you feel numb. Fr. Whelan must have had novocaine. Because after a minute, I was numb. He had the same expressionless face as the dentist did when he jabbed me with the novocaine. I could smell the novocaine on Whelan, or the dentist, I don't know who it was, but I couldn't feel what they were doing anymore.

That feeling of knowing your body is being tampered with and pulled and scraped and violated in different ways, while your flesh has been deliberately deprived of its ability to warn you of the invasion, is so unnatural.

A Witch Wins JUSTICE

You realize that when the novocaine wears off you're going to suffer, and you just wait for the inevitable.

As usual, Jesus sat there on the wall and did absolutely nothing. He stared at me as though he did me a favor by letting Whelan use some kind of hidden novocaine. I watched as novocaine dripped from Jesus' mouth, and he seemed so proud that he had allowed the diabolical liquid to be invented. He couldn't speak clearly because the novocaine made his own mouth numb, so I didn't really hear what he had to say. It would have been worthless anyway. Jesus can be so rotten and insensitive. So can the dentist, so can Whelan, all because of that goddamn novocaine.

I tried to keep my eyes closed and forget about the whole thing, but every time I opened my eyes there I was, back in Whelan's office, and the dentist wasn't even around. Novocaine still dripped from Jesus' mouth while he hung on the wall and smiled, and I was hoping He would choke on it.

Go ahead Jesus, please choke, maybe that will wake you up to what's going on.

Jesus let the novocaine drip down from his mouth, down his body, down the cross he was on, and then the novocaine dripped down the wall. He thought it was amusing. I couldn't stand to watch him; I just looked away.

Then the novocaine wore off. I was stuck there.

Now I had a new problem—Whelan had graduated to getting physically and sexually violent. I didn't know what to do.

But then came the salt. The saltwater was back. It had been years since the saltwater leaked out of my eyes to save me; I had forgotten about it. It leaked down my face into my mouth like I expected it to. It tasted odd, mixed with novocaine. There was no sink to spit the novocaine and drool into. The dentist's office was rearranged.

I fought back the saltwater tears; I was too old now, I thought. And Whelan was unsympathetic.

I managed to blurb out something like, "I told you."

But the poisonous priest still looked as though he had venom in his eyes. I was scared. I was worried. What I really wanted was to get the hell out of Salesian High School as fast as I could at that very second. But I knew it was futile. I was trapped.

Somehow, in a blur, I left the room numbly that day, while Whelan coldly stared at me.

He let me leave without reaction, probably because he knew I was not going to do or say anything.

It was hard to concentrate on schoolwork at that time. Everything was turning ugly, just like Whelan and his big ugly horse gum-chewing face.

Although I didn't fully understand why this was happening to me at the time, I was resenting my religion, I was resenting my school, and I was resenting God. I was transforming from the happy grade-A student into somebody I hated. Somebody who let this all happen. Somebody who I thought was a coward, a fool, and a hypocrite. And a poor excuse for a man. Not only that, I was a poor excuse for a boy.

No wonder I was Fr. Whelan's Bitch.

I stopped praying at night, because I was mad at God. He was lazy. He thought novocaine was the answer to the problem. It wasn't. God was wrong, and he was not doing his job like he used to when I was a child.

A Witch Wins JUSTICE

No wonder He failed and they crucified him. I had hoped they crucified him without novocaine. I had thought he deserved it, for helping Whelan.

I started to skip going to church on Sunday, and I would lie to my parents and tell them I was still going. I started to see the dark side of things, and the drawings I drew were now mostly sick, disturbing, and twisted. It was as if I was fighting to keep my old personality, but the new me was a tormented soul who intruded, and wanted to be different, and liked to be confused and angry, looking for the bad in the world around me.

Maybe I was a werewolf. A normal person turning into a demon.

I was having nightmares I couldn't understand, and weird headaches at all different hours. I began to have the nightmares of the witch tortures and burnings again, and I saw visions of fragments of some sort of trial. I could see more details of the wicked "chamber" and the flashes of some sort of interrogation or tribunal. It was difficult to piece together the stories, because the scenes were out of order. It was as though I was speeding through a video of a movie and stopping at random, going forward and backward without justification. It seemed to be an addition to my dreams I had as a child, memories I had forgotten about years ago. They were back again.

The nightmares were filled with people like Whelan, authorities without feeling, torturing innocent people without regard to morals or ethics, and they were holding the trials. They seemed much more realistic and vivid now, and it was hard to shake them.

Into the Salesian High School of Horrors

I had to wake up each day and return to the school of horrors and face it all again.

And I felt like I had a dirty little secret with Fr. Whelan and like it was all my doing. The inner conflict was confusing to say the least; sometimes I would just pretend that nothing was wrong at all, and other times I felt like a bomb of sickness had dropped on me. Sometimes I imagined that God, Whelan, and I were all the same; sick bastards with sick secrets. I had joined a sick club of losers, without them giving me a choice.

I knew I couldn't ask God for help; it was obvious he was a part of it.

It was probably at this point in my life that I first became interested in learning about "the occult," which was a mysterious and completely unknown subject to me at the time. The confused mental state I had been introduced to by the defective Catholic priest caused me to question the nature of true spirituality. Perhaps, I thought, exploring other forms of belief systems, which had been "off-limits" my entire life up to this point, was something I would look into in the near future.

The small bit of investigating into the "occult" that I did at the time was a surprise. I learned that Shamanism, Buddhism, and "alternative beliefs" I had been told were the evil works of the Devil were in fact not evil Satanist cults, and I wondered why I had been misled all of my life. Unfortunately, I had little time to investigate these new revelations; I had a predator to fight off. But I felt so drawn to a different path that it seemed much more than a diversion; it felt as though it was a return to something I could not explain.

And then came the "stairway meetings."

A Witch Wins JUSTICE

Whelan would know when I would be on the stairs. God must have told him, I guessed. God was very sneaky that way. He hung around Whelan's neck and told him everywhere I would be. God and Whelan both had a thing for the stairs.

And Whelan was always angry with me. I couldn't figure out just why; maybe it was because he loathed our dirty little secrets and he blamed me for the sins. There was one time when he snuck up behind me and I didn't know it. I was going up the stairs, and I thought I felt something behind me—I wasn't sure, and I turned around, and there he was, his face touching my butt. I don't know if he was smelling me or trying to kiss my butt, as weird and depraved as it sounds.

"What are you doing?" I yelled.

He became very angry and started pinching me hard, and he grabbed me between my legs. I was so completely shocked, I think I screamed. I can't remember clearly my exact words—I was spacing out, but I told him he was hurting me. He then disappeared as quickly as he had appeared.

The goddamn novocaine wore off before it had time to take effect. God was playing tricks on me again.

Things calmed down a bit after that, and Whelan would see me around the school, and he acted as though nothing at all was happening. Almost as though he had totally forgotten. I wished I could have forgotten. Life at this time was confusing enough without the new game he was playing, acting as though he didn't even know I existed and pretending that all was normal.

Maybe that's how a werewolf lives. Pretending everything is normal, and then turning into the monster when he decides to. God isn't funny. I never thought he was. I always prayed like a good boy, and this is how he rewarded me? Mommy was wrong about him. But it wasn't her fault. She had been fooled too. Maybe there was still some kind of chance to salvage what was left of my faith. Maybe there were some priests who weren't werewolves or demons.

That was it. Maybe a confession was in order. The last chance.

The school had mass and church services sometimes, and I decided to go to confession at the school when it was offered one day. I had not been to confession in a while, and I thought I was long overdue. I had a lot of baggage and crap to get off my chest. I told myself this could be a turning point in the right direction. Maybe God would have a change of heart, and become normal again, and be the God I used to trust and love. I felt I was man enough to forgive God for all of his deceptive bullshit and make the good faith leap back into the Catholic sacramental voyage.

I entered the confessional and knelt down and carefully said,

"Bless me Father, for I have sinned. And these are my sins."

I had to wait a minute. I guess there was too long of a silence, but I didn't know where to begin, and if I should be "ratting out" Fr. Steve Whelan to one of his buddies. I was debating how to disclose the horror story, or if I would even mention the issue at all, when the priest broke the long silence.

The priest behind the screen said, "Go on."

I couldn't tell who the priest was. His voice was muffled. But an eerie thought came over me. What if the priest listening on the other side in the confessional was Whelan? I didn't know. I had second thoughts. I had to leave. I started to panic. The priest spoke again.

"Go ahead," he said. I still couldn't tell who it was.

"I don't think I'm ready," I said.

Then I felt stupid. What a ridiculous thing to say, I thought. Couldn't I have thought of something more intelligent?

The priest interrupted my thoughts.

"Well, I am sure there must be something that you want to tell me."

His voice was still too muffled, and I was still unable to determine who he was. As I strained to see who the cleric was on the other side of the barrier, that familiar smell of alcohol-fumed breath, which I had first been exposed to in a confessional in early childhood, had permeated the barrier and been identified by my senses. The smell of oak wood, the blend of alcohol and an aged confessional box filled my head. I felt dizzy.

God was at it again.

He could do it; He could do anything. Why did He have it in for me like this? I was just about to turn myself around and come back to Him, to forgive Him, and He pulls this shit.

I was just contemplating getting up and running out of the confessional when the priest spoke up again.

"Well let me ask you, how often do you touch yourself?" he said calmly.

I couldn't believe it. Who was this priest? Whelan? Or is there another one who is just like him? Did he know who I was? And why would a priest ask me that?

Into the Salesian High School of Horrors

I wanted to get up and leave. The confessional grew pitch black and smelled like alcohol again. Suddenly I was blind. I tried to feel my way by touching the walls, and I closed my eyes and leaned backward and fell through a door in the side of the confessional, and entered the dark atmosphere. I think I had fallen asleep, or maybe I was unconscious. I was eleven again, and I looked up and saw my Uncle Frank, at the Christmas party, and he had been drinking. He stank of alcohol and confessional wood. He hugged me and told me that I should run away whenever I smelled alcohol on a priest. Fr. Tollner was behind him, listening in, trying to hand me a beer. Uncle Frank knew it and told me to get out of the confessional; it smelled too much like alcohol.

He was right. Run.

I got up in the dark room, blindly, and I made my way to the door and left. I never answered the priest.

That was the last time I ever went to confession in my life.

By now I'd had more than my share of the Salesian nightmare. Where does it end? Am I the only one? School was like a very sour episode of *The Twilight Zone*, and I was in the middle of too much religion-gone-bad scenes. I wanted out. Maybe my confusion was turning to misguided aggression at this point, because I was getting into trouble with my sarcasm and comments in the classroom more often now. As fate would have it, I was sent down to the office. And of course, Whelan was there. And he was so excited to see me. He told me to sit down on the chair by the desk.

The horrible Salesian cycle of terror yet again. Another kick in the ass by *The Twilight Zone* religion series.

A Witch Wins JUSTICE

I shook my head as I walked in, thinking of how it would look to all of my relatives hearing that I dropped out of high school. Would that be an alternative? What do kids do when they are in my shoes?

Whelan shut the door to the office. Or was it the chamber? It was both.

"You're really in trouble now," he smiled that perverse smile of his.

He pulled up a chair next to mine and faced me, looking into my eyes.

"You're going to get kicked out of school," he continued, "and I am the only one who can save you." "Do you understand that? I just looked back at him. I said nothing. He was enjoying this. I could tell he was getting sexually excited and that it was another move in the same game. I was never good at games; my brothers and sisters always beat me at games, probably because I really wasn't into it. I was bad at pool, bad at Ping-Pong, and bad at baseball.

And now I was bad at "Dodge the Priest." This game was worse, but my track record for losing games was consistent.

"What are you going to do for me?" he asked, almost drooling on himself.

"What do you mean?" was all I could answer. But I did not want to know what he meant.

"What are you going to do for me?" he demanded, getting louder.

He was getting uneasy now, and angrier.

"I'm the only one who can save you from getting kicked out of school, do you understand that? So what are you going to do for me?"

Into the Salesian High School of Horrors

I knew what he meant now. Why play stupid. I'm going to lose the game either way, whether stupid or smart, whether participating or not—none of it mattered. I was destined to lose the games with Whelan and God.

I could read his snarl, the wrinkles around his nose and mouth, the sickness in his eyes, that horse gum with those horse teeth and mouth. I could also read those big wolf eyebrows and that phony white priest collar, probably made out of phony bread, that matched the phony white Communion wafer.

Behind him on the wall, Jesus was watching again, but I'd learned by now that He had abandoned me. I knew whose side He was on. This had happened too many times for me to ask Him for any help. Jesus dangled from Whelan's neck too. How convenient for the two of them. The inseparable twins.

Why couldn't Whelan swallow the Jesus necklace and choke to death on Him?

No such luck.

Whelan spoke up again. Then he put his hand on my thigh.

"I asked you a question, now answer me." He demanded, looking down at his hand on my thigh.

"I don't know," I said. "But I'm leaving."

I stood up to leave, and Whelan became livid. He could not believe I would defy him at this point.

"Don't you dare leave," he yelled. "I will have you thrown out of school."

I headed for the door. I was daring him, and he knew it. It had finally come to this. Then he threw me another curve ball.

A Witch Wins JUSTICE

"You don't think anybody is going to believe your word against a priest, do you?"
I turned back in shock. So this was what it was about. I finally grew a brain. The new game was an exchange game. He wanted me to engage in some perverted act with him in exchange for my staying in tact at school, and if I told on him, he would deny it, and no one would believe me. So the rules changed a bit; if you feel you are losing the game, you can't just walk out and quit, like kids often do.

Quitting wasn't allowed.

In a split second I realized two things. The first, I'd rather get kicked out than have perverted sex with the creep. The second thing was that I thought he was right. No one would believe my word against a priest. I hesitated, and then I walked out. I was going to quit and face the consequences of being a sore loser and a quitter.

For several days after that, I waited for someone to drop the bomb on me, but it didn't happen. Maybe things would cool down. But my performance was declining. And my anger and sarcasm in class was continuing. And I was bound to end up in his office again somehow.

The next time I saw Fr. Whelan, he acted again as though nothing happened. But I definitely had absolutely no trust in him whatsoever, or in any other priest for that matter. Or God.

Or Gum. Or novocaine.

I just wanted to somehow graduate and get as far away as I could from that school. Then, the inevitable happened. I got in trouble again for being a wise ass in class and was sent down to the office again. It was

Into the Salesian High School of Horrors

the same repetitious, vicious cycle: the more Whelan disturbed me, the more I acted out, and the more I got in trouble.

And of course, quitting was not allowed.

Whelan saw me at his office door and told me to meet him by the stairs when school was over that day.

He seemed unemotional, and he said I was in bad trouble, and I was even more skeptical about his demeanor this time.

It was one of those days that I was sure I shouldn't meet him after school. I was just beginning to think that if I avoided him, everything would go away. But there I was, at the foot of the stairs, by the central office hall, and I could still hear him telling me minutes ago that I was in bad trouble. Trouble for what, I really didn't care. It didn't matter; it was bound to keep happening. His face was stuck in my head, and his eyes were not erasable, although I tried so hard to destroy that picture in my head.

And then there was the smell of starch.

That's what I thought it was. It reminded me of him. Every time in the past when he grabbed me, or touched me, I smelled starch on his black clothes. It got to the point that I believed the color black was made of dark starch. And it was evil starch. It permeated the room like the smoke in the chamber.

My mom had used starch when she ironed, throughout my childhood, and it never was a smell I associated with fear. But now it was. Now I hated it. I was staring at the staircase when that smell of vulgar starch crawled into my head from behind me. I turned slowly around, and for a few seconds I imagined I could hold my breath and the starch would disappear, and so would Fr. Whelan. But God must have been in a bad mood again.

"Get up the stairs," Whelan commanded, breaking the silence coldly.

"Where are we going?" I managed to cough out.

"We're going to the multipurpose room on the third floor," he barked, and he held his big hand pointed toward the stairway.

"Get up there!" he jumped, and I scattered like a puppy.

Between the complete confusion as to why we were headed toward the "multipurpose room" on the third floor, and the growing contempt in his voice, I didn't notice I was being grabbed from behind. All of a sudden it hit me that this had already happened before. Fr. Whelan had met me before on the stairway, not long before this, and had grabbed me between the legs, and I had tried to dismiss it as a bad incident that goes away like a dog bite that heals with time.

But this time was worse. The dog bites were bigger and more painful. I could feel his big hand slapping my butt hard, and I didn't think it hurt that much, but I turned to see his face, and I knew the distorted expression on his mask wasn't normal. It was as though it hurt him to slap my butt, and he winced each time, and his huge eyebrows wrinkled like he was sneering at a dead animal. His eyes were glowing red. The werewolf was back.

I turned away, and I seemed to take each step on the stairs without feeling my foot land but knowing I was ascending toward the third floor. It was then I felt a sharp stinging pain between my legs, and I lost my breath when I realized that his finger was pushing into my butt and that he was pinching me at the same time. I felt the blood drain from my face, and for an instant I thought that this couldn't be happening, I was going to wake up soon; and at the same time I had the horrific thought pop into my head for the first time in my life that God was really the Devil.

That's what this was about.

God was really the devil, and it had taken this long for me to learn that. I should have realized that much earlier than this; there were so many signs.

As I continued to head up the stairs, thinking of why it took me so long to realize that God was the devil, I started to feel myself "float."

I lost sense of time at this point, and it seemed as though his disgusting finger was there for an hour, although it must have been seconds. It didn't occur to me to question why he pushed so hard through my pants and was able to do what he did, and I felt myself drifting away.

The floating was more strange than frightful, and I tried to maintain my senses when I started to see him pinching me from what appeared to be a side view. I was actually watching him and me, ascending up the stairs as though I was a third person. Then I was back on the stairs. Dammit.

I snapped back out of whatever was causing me to do this, and I managed to blurt out, "You're hurting me!"

As if Whelan gave a shit. His response was more disturbing.

"You've been a bad boy. Now get up there!"

Somehow, the stair climb seemed to take days, and I felt like I'd started at the bottom again and that time

A Witch Wins JUSTICE

had shifted backward. Then when I would ascend to the top of the stairway, I was back at the bottom again, starting over.

I can't count how many times he slapped me, or penetrated me with his finger, although I remember getting to the top of the stairs somehow. But the rabid priest was relentless. He was pinching me even when I was disappearing and watching from five feet away. He couldn't tell when I was gone; he kept attacking my ghost. But I kept coming back to the stairs.

If ever there was an incident in my life that was a testament to the unspeakable horror of certain doom brought on by the Almighty himself, it was now. My uncontrollable fright was now complete chaos. Fr. Whelan was attacking me like a sadistic rapist, and I started to float away yet again.

Although I appreciated leaving the stairs while this was happening, I could still see broken flashes of him grabbing me from what appeared to be above the stairway, five feet away. I saw myself, and the priest, from above, then I must have been ten feet way, watching him, and watching me, and it was like a slow motion picture from a broken camera. The muffled confusion I was watching below was hard to decipher. I thought my head would hit the high ceiling of the stairway as I was floating so far above, but I never felt myself bang the ceiling.

The horror unfolded sporadically, and my sense of hearing disappeared. So did my sense of feeling. I couldn't feel any pain, and I don't remember breathing. For split-second pulses I was there, then gone, and I believed my body was disintegrating, and I was accepting the fact that I must be dying. I left the stairway altogether and went back to the torture chamber again, hundreds of years ago, and I saw blood splatter that I had not noticed before, and new church interrogators.

I thought that the interrogators didn't notice I had left the torture chamber and returned. Or maybe they did. Perhaps that's why they thought I was a witch—I was able to disappear and return, in and out of time, right before their eyes. I understood now why they thought I had strange powers as a witch, because they knew I could leave the interrogation and go somewhere into the future, and return again, and disappear again, and it gave them validation that I was guilty of witchcraft.

They were going to torture me again, so I left them again.

It was like changing the channels from one station to another, in slow motion, and watching clips of myself as a witch being tortured, and then watching the trial, and then watching myself being molested. But now, the Witch trial had altered. The trial chamber was different. It appeared as though it was now a modern trial, with modern people, in a modern courtroom. The old trial in the chamber had been replaced. Where the hell was I now?

Then came the salt. It finally was flowing down my face, and it ran down into my mouth. It was time to wake and run to Mommy.

I ran into Mommy's room crying, and she was sleeping. But I couldn't wake her up. I kept nudging her arm, and she wouldn't open her eyes. So I pushed harder, and my hand went through her arm. That's when it hit me: she wasn't there. I was so angry with her. She said she would always be there for me, and now she was gone. I couldn't go back to bed—my bedroom was gone too; I had to go back to the stairway.

When I got back to the stairway with Whelan, I could feel my heart beating loudly in my ears. Whelan was dragging my soulless body into the multipurpose room. But it was really the old chamber again. He must have known the whole time. I knew that this was the proper introduction to death in hell. The nuns had always talked about it. It wasn't hot like they said. They had always been guessing, they never really knew what hell was like. They must have never known Whelan.

It was cold, and there was cold blood seeping out from the walls, from crevices and other places.

Cold blood is thicker, like a good-quality paint.

It is perfect for artwork. I was part of the artwork, there was no mistake.

Then it was remarkably peaceful for a few minutes. It was resplendent and serene, and there was a drizzling calm, damp mist. What a relief.

Sometimes blood is so pretty.

The garnet and deep red colors feel so awkward when you're numb, and gravity pulls the trails down your skin like a thin, carefully guided paintbrush. But each shiny trail creates swirls and angles by itself, painting an exquisite pathway until it decides to drip somewhere, a place it has chosen at random; droplets of lovely crimson become glistening art, its creator losing a small amount of liquid life, one droplet at a time. But that loss is for the sake of beautiful art, a collateral effect of the trade.

It's hard to duplicate. God really is an exquisite artist, I thought, who teaches priests to paint like this, and children's blood is such a delicate, fascinating medium.

I seemed to have completely forgotten how cold it was in the chamber, as I had been consumed by watching the incredible painting unfold.

I flew around the room, watching the two artists at work, Fr. Whelan and God, busy creating their masterpiece of timeless, bloody distortion. But it was impossible to not notice the intense and desperate screaming in the distance, which kept getting louder.

For me, it interrupted the observation of the creation of the artistic masterpiece. The witches were melting in the fires, and the artists were too busy to hear them, but the shrieking pierced my ears and penetrated my head beyond toleration.

As would be expected, the remarkable peacefulness had to come to an end.

I really needed to go back home.

Unfortunately, it was getting much too dark, and when I stopped flying and landed on the floor, it was very difficult to walk, because I kept slipping on the bloody floor. The artists had not cleaned up yet; perhaps they still had work to do. But I couldn't wait anymore, I left the art room, groping in the dark.

I went back to seeing myself again, in the multi purpose room minutes later, but all I could see was God himself raping me, sadistically, in what felt more like an accident-inspired mutilation than any artwork. His style had changed. He was wearing Whelan's clothes, as if to fool me.

The artwork was being destroyed; all that arduous preparation and talent was for nothing. I could see God with an erection, pissing blood in my face, and I tasted starch, blood, and vomit. The vomit ruined the painting. I

A Witch Wins JUSTICE

do not know how long it lasted, and I do not know where Fr. Whelan was at this point. Why God would choose vomit to mix with blood as a medium for the artwork was perplexing. It was counterproductive.

He should know better.

I do not know how God switched clothes with Whelan or why they continued their charade. It was then I must have fallen asleep, thinking I was dead, or perhaps exhausted from the art lesson. I do not even remember waking, or leaving, or how I got home. How I hated them both.

I finally realized God wasn't really a gifted artist. He was a phony. He was an accomplice of Whelan, who created inferior artwork, taking credit for disguised art, which in actuality was truly poor craftsmanship. Their teamwork and apprenticeship was detestable.

I went to experience the other movies instead. Luckily, in the darkness of the room, time had stopped, and I was able to travel to what was my past life, and since time was irrelevant, and I was so close to death anyway, I witnessed more of the witch trial I was in hundreds of years ago. I surprised the interrogators by returning; I needed to gather as much information as the absence of time would allow, as it would be important in the future.

Thank you weird merciless God, for the opportunity you presented.

I saw things that I had not seen before: frightening images of torture and wicked interrogators from the past, and scenes of the chamber room that were much more vivid in detail and color. I understood what to expect now.

Into the Salesian High School of Horrors

Perhaps trauma is the very best key to past-life recall there could possibly be, nudging prior memories to the surface to be viewed like an exceptionally well-directed movie. The absence of time was clearly a valuable contributor, as it demonstrated that the illusion of life isn't past-life retrieval, the illusion of life is the lack of the ability to remember the hidden past.

I know the experience at the time of the attack of leaving the body and floating is very similar to the floating experience I had dreams about as a child, where I was watching myself from the sky full of stars, and there was no sensation of sound, or pain, or time. That experience I remembered as a child was the reality. I had discovered the key to its existence.

However, even though trauma may cause you to "leave your body," so to speak, it is usually not willful, but I understand it is a defense mechanism by the unconscious to protect the mind from harm. The altered states caused by trauma also have similarities to intentional altered states practiced by Magickians, but that practice is a favorable one, and obviously a better circumstance in ritual. I realized my traumas in both lives cooperated with each other in an exchange, and the result of Karma was yet to be determined.

I was predestined to learn these lessons, although the circumstances were not exhilarating.

I cannot count how many nights I have jumped out of bed at three in the morning, reliving the multipurpose room scene, realizing I had literally stopped breathing, and catching my breath. I would actually taste the blood and vomit again. I would see Fr. Whelan's hands

A Witch Wins JUSTICE

with blood on them, I would see his frightened face, and I would be scared to sleep.

But that horrific day in 1970 wasn't over.

The next scene I can remember from that day was when I walked into the hallway bathroom at my house in Richmond. My house was probably five miles away from Salesian High School, and I still do not know how I got there or what time I got home. There was an eerie hissing in my ears, not unlike the fuzzy humming sound you experience after a loud concert. I had a dull headache, and I could feel myself tremble, but yet I was numb, as if my legs had fallen asleep.

It was unclear to me who was in control of my senses, but I went through the motion of pulling down my pants, as if I were being controlled remotely by someone else. It was like an unseen person, who was unknown to me, was directing my body to do certain tasks without my permission. Then I lowered my underwear. The hiss in my ears changed to a ringing. The ringing morphed quickly into a loud heartbeat in my eardrums, like what had occurred on the dreaded stairway to hell earlier that day.

The blood was still wet.

My white underwear had blood in it, which perfectly matched the red stripe on the waistband of my cotton briefs. I tasted the starch in my throat but wasn't sure if it was really vomit; I had somehow blended the two together as one taste, and my ability to distinguish had been altered.

I will never use starch again for any reason. Maybe I had swallowed the necklace of Jesus, and it was made of starch, and it had caused me to vomit. I tried to throw

Into the Salesian High School of Horrors

up Jesus, to get him out of my system, but it didn't happen. Perhaps that is why I still feel like vomiting whenever I am near a church.

In any case, I snuck quietly into my bedroom and shut the door. Instinctively I took another pair of underwear out of the drawer, stuck it up my shirt, walked briskly out the front door of the house, and went into the shed house we had built in our backyard.

I don't know why, or what drove me to this point, but I changed into the clean underwear as fast as possible. I couldn't let anyone see. I felt as guilty as if I had just killed somebody, and I knew I had to bury the body as soon as I could. I didn't stop to think of what had happened, or how I got home; I had to dispose of the underwear now.

I peeked outside the shed to see if the coast was clear, and went over to the side of the shed to search for a rock. What motivated me to choose a rock for the disposal was a mystery. I remember the rock well. It was about five inches long by about three inches wide, and it seemed heavy for its size. I speculated it might be iron or something. It didn't matter; it was the right size and shape and weight.

I wrapped the bloody underwear around the rock and tied it as best as I could. Walking over toward the fence, I made the best throw I could, and sent the rock sailing over the fence as far as I thought was possible. There was a swamp behind the fence, and I was sure that the rock would take the underwear into the muddy ground, never to be seen again.

I was relieved to have gotten rid of the evidence of the artwork of God and his protégé Whelan. When I turned around, I saw my dog, Snoopy, staring at me.

A Witch Wins JUSTICE

Snoopy had been my dog for seven years, and lived in the yard, and had always been a loyal and faithful, loving companion. She would never tell a soul. I could see the pity in her eyes; she understood I was in pain. I hugged Snoopy after I had thrown the rock of my spiritual death artwork over the fence, and she watched the saltwater trickle down my face, and she knew what had happened. She was always a clever dog, this mutt, and I had always felt her unconditional love. God could have learned so much from her. She was much better to me than God had ever been, and I loved her in return.

Unfortunately she died a few years later, after being hit by a car. I will never forget the look in her eyes when she passed on; it was a look of desperation, a look of finality. There is a film that covers the eyes of a living creature at the moment of death, eyes wide open that stare into the horizon, a blank stare that mesmerizes and hypnotizes the observer into an understanding of that final perception of loss of life, a look that remains in the eyes of the deceased. And that glaze of thin film coats the eyes as the creature enters the atmosphere. It is truly unforgettable. I remember seeing that glaze in my cousin Curt's eyes, and in the eyes of the burning witches. And hideously, in my own mirror.

After I went back into my house, I took the crucifix of Jesus off the bedroom wall, and it somehow crumbled into pieces on the floor. It could have been me breaking it, I don't recall clearly, but I couldn't stand looking at the phony artist anymore, staring at me as though nothing had happened. I threw the broken pieces in the garbage where they belonged, and buried Him with no eulogy or apology. I looked down into the garbage can, and it appeared as though the broken pieces of Jesus resembled the vomit.

It made sense now: I understood the connection between God, Whelan, and throwing up.

It was years later that I decided to go back and search for the rock. Of course I couldn't find it—the swamp had been dredged many times by then, and the forces of nature had altered the swamp dramatically. It was my way of searching for the corpse of my soul. In an eerie way I thought the bad God who raped me made me hide my own spiritual death.

I was pretty sure that God went back and got the rock for his trophy and that he had it on his mantle in some evil chamber. I could see him going back after I threw the rock in the swamp, laughing hysterically at the way I had tied my bloody underwear around it, and telling Whelan how stupid I was for thinking I could hide it from Him, who is all-knowing and all-seeing. They probably took turns playing with the rock and hid it in the church. They truly deserved each other.

The days and weeks after the horrible attack on the stairway and multipurpose room were gloomy, and numbing, and I do not know how I did any class work, if I did any at all. I would arrive at school, and go through the motions of getting books out of my locker and attending class, and have the feeling that life was the same as it was before the attacks. Then I would find myself staring off into nowhere, and having a feeling when I stopped staring that I had been in a daze for hours. I would lose track of time, and leave one class after it ended, and forget which class to go to next.

A Witch Wins JUSTICE

Sometimes I would forget what time of day it was, and think I had not been to a class that I had just left five minutes before. Later on in the day, I would see classwork in my binder that I had completed the same day, and not recognize it. This was frightening, as I began to think I was losing perceptibility and being uncontrollably disconnected. One of the horrors of this intermittent pattern was finding pictures that I had drawn of myself being molested, and not having any recollection of drawing them earlier that same day. The first time this happened, I assumed that someone had placed the drawing into my binder somehow, without me noticing. Then, after examining the picture, I would recognize the characters in the picture as myself, and the despicable priest, and occasionally God. I would realize at this point that no one else could have drawn them but me, and the thought would be terrorizing.

This bizarre behavior would cease, and then resume again at a different time. I do not know the length of time this behavior lasted, but on some days I withdrew completely and would have involuntary flashes of what appeared to be still photographs of some kind of hideous accident. And I would have more memories of early childhood, and the dreams I told my mother about, concerning the Witch burnings.

I felt like I was somehow mentally short-circuiting at that time, as I kept having the same type of unwanted flashes of the accident like scenes, and flashes of God, Whelan, and pictures that did not make any sense whatsoever. Then, I would feel as though I had just woken up, and that nothing had happened, it was all just a bad dream. But that feeling would dissolve, and I would recall regretting going up the stairway with Whelan, and I would realize it was not a bad dream; it was all too real.

I repeatedly had split-second flashes of the horror on Whelan's' face, during the attack, and my recollection tells me that he was scared of what he had done. Whelan disappeared not too long after that attack and did not return to Salesian High School that I know of. I do remember briefly seeing him at different places at the school, and I could see that if he caught the slightest glimpse of me, he would turn and go in the opposite direction or look away as though he never saw me. Of course I was glad that he was avoiding me, as I was definitely avoiding him too. But what was bewildering about this at the same time was the fact that *I* felt guilty. It was a strange guilt, unlike the guilt I had felt at other times in my life where I had broken something, or hit my brother as a child, or did anything to deserve any of the common guilt feelings a child has.

This guilt was horror guilt.

A wicked sensation of guilt one might associate with doing something detestable and gruesome. I could not rationalize why I myself felt so much guilt. This unexplainable guilt brought with it an urge to hide from everyone, terrified someone would expose me. Watching Whelan hide from me as he did added to my anguish, because I was doing the same thing, and it reinforced the disturbing thought that we were both guilty of the same crime together. It never occurred to me that victims blame themselves sometimes; I was unaware of the things that were happening to me. I did not know that sex abuse victims have flashbacks, anxiety, insomnia, and other disorders; I lived through them all, not knowing the psychological damage that was done to me.

I never told my friends about the abuse. I couldn't bring up the courage. And they all seemed to be doing so well "growing up." So why mention how weird I was, and the unspeakable horror I was living. Perhaps it was the resilience of youth, or perhaps I was denying this nightmare the chance to engulf me entirely, but I continued living and going to school. I was a changed person—that was evident, and I struggled with studies and schoolwork, and my "Christian" spirituality had completely melted away. Most of all, I was determined to hide all the dirty secrets, absolutely convinced that "no one will believe your word against a priest."

After the Molester Disappeared

Fr. Whelan disappeared from Salesians shortly after the attacks, and it is my belief that he asked to have himself removed and sent somewhere else because he did not want to be caught or discovered. Brother Sal Billante, who had witnessed the instances of abuse by Whelan at the Boys Club, disappeared at about the same time. Perhaps a Salesian official removed them both and separated them from the high school because of a complaint by another victim.

I had hoped that they were both killed in a tragic plane crash at the time and that I would see it on the news.

That never happened. Dammit.

It is not impossible to imagine that the Salesians would have conveniently lost any and all evidence and records of the deeds of these two unconscionable sex offender twins, and disposed of them long ago. I found out years later that Whelan was sent to Canada at some point, which seems to be something the Salesians have been accused of before, as I have read: to transfer their predators to other countries, far away from their crime scenes. Little did I know at the time that Bro. Sal Billante was an egregious serial molester, had molested several boys at the Boys Club, and had numerous victims at other Salesian locations as well. Billante was in the habit of taking nude photographs of naked young boys,

A Witch Wins JUSTICE

and I think he showed them to other pedophiles, and possibly he may have had the opportunity to share them with Whelan. Billante is also said to have had victims who have committed suicide.

It was no wonder to me then, that Whelan felt so comfortable masturbating in front of Billante. Sal Billante was later convicted of sexual molestation, spending several years in prison. It was no surprise to me when I found out that Billante and Whelan had grown up together and had been very close since early in their own childhood. The unforgivable acts they both committed against children are inconceivable. Perhaps that is why they were removed simultaneously.

During my high school years, the priests and brothers of Salesian High slept in a large residence building on the Salesian school grounds, and several other Salesian clergy from other areas had lived there also. Later accusations and lawsuits showed that a record number of Salesian clergy living there were named as sexual molesters.

What is remarkable is the life style of the Salesian priests and brothers, the crimes that many of them committed, and the fact that they stayed so loyal to each other, never betraying each other's trust.

I returned to Salesian my junior year, and with both Whelan and Billante "gone," I kept struggling to complete my junior and senior year to try to graduate. But not without an entire new set of unwanted problems. I was absolutely convinced that God, whoever he was, wanted me dead for all I had caused. So I kept telling myself I did not believe in God, but I still believed that somehow he might exist in some form and that he was going to get revenge to punish me for the artwork that was flawed and destroyed. He was also going to punish me for being a witch, and visiting the chamber, and leaving during the abuse to escape into the afterlife.

I never forgave God, or Jesus, or Fr. Whelan. In my head they were inseparable, one and all the same. Like the Father, Son, and Holy Spirit of the Catholic faith.

A long series of incredible nightmares and memories continued after the last abuse incident, and so did a relentless invasion of headaches, depression, insomnia, and self-loathing.

The confusion I felt as a devout Catholic, who had been raised to firmly believe in God and all that is sacred, was overwhelming. For my entire life before the abuse by Whelan, I had accepted the "undeniable truth" that God had created me, and that was indisputable.

I began to have stomach problems and to experience anxiety, and I was afraid to tell anybody why.

Fortunately, or unfortunately—I didn't know which, I started to go to "parties" on the weekends. I became much more interested in life outside of high school than life at Salesian High.

If you could call it life.

I needed some kind of outlet; whether or not it may have been caustic was not important. The confusion of teenage years definitely becomes much more complicated to those who were molested by perverse adults. The hit-and-miss journey through adolescence is rocky enough without the added task of hiding the effects of invisible wounds that have ripped a person's soul apart.

I thought I noticed that people who drank alcohol and smoked pot for recreation on Friday and Saturday nights were much happier than I was. Sure, it was wrong, and they were underage, but so what? If the "closest person on earth to God," a priest, was a sexual pervert, and God had no problem with that, then who the hell cared? The rationalization here was: if there really was a God, and his priests were rabid perpetrators with no conscience, than getting smashed on weekends was a minor infraction which could be easily forgiven and forgotten.

The tumultuous life of an abuse victim predisposes the person to self-destructive behavior, and the blending of desperation and risk becomes inviting. The desire for me to leave the real world was overpowering.

So I drank. I partied. I smoked pot. I took to heart the lyrics to the song "The Watchtower." In the immortal words of Jimi Hendrix and Bobby Dylan, both of whom I idolized at the time,

> *There must be some kind of way out of here, said the joker to the thief…there's too much confusion, I can't get no relief…*

I've often heard it said that the music people listen to at certain times in their early lives stimulates emotions that can be recalled and relived years later. Many of us know this to be true. And I can still relive the times when I attended parties and drank with friends years ago as a young teenager, when I hear that same music. But I can also retrieve the bittersweet, anguished desire to somehow escape the disappointing reality that twisted fate had dumped on me.

It became a weekend ritual in high school to go to parties every weekend and get blitzed with my friends. I,

After the Molester Disappeared

for one, could not think of another way out at the time. And it was consoling that I had company. Without knowing the other kids' reasons for their escape, I was content to know that at least during the weekends, I was not alone.

The self-medicating rituals of drinking and smoking seemed endless, and in a recalcitrant way, it seemed justified. Besides, it seemed as though many of my friends looked forward to the same thing, only their grades weren't slipping like mine. Sadly, this pattern was my only "relief" at the time. As fate would have it, I seemed to be sending more and more of my anxiety at the time to my stomach.

After all, it had to go somewhere.

After a while my mother had noticed I was having stomach problems, and she took me to the doctor. The doctor sent me to the hospital for barium tests. The tests showed negative. He then told me in so many words that I might be experiencing an emotional or psychological disorder. I told my mother the doctor was crazy, that he did not know what he was talking about. But the stomach problems persisted, and I was given some kind of medicine to calm me down. I would never tell my mother and father about my problems with Whelan: it was unthinkable.

It was in my junior year that I met my first real girlfriend. She was attractive and slender, and a year younger than me. We were a good match at the time, as I was a lost soul, and neither of us ever stopped to think about what a lost soul was or where a lost soul goes. I believe she may have been a lost soul also, although we never discussed the psychological reasons for the compatibility in this area. We weren't capable of that kind of analytical dialogue.

It was unimportant, because we liked each other, and we may have even loved each other; but at the very least, we both understood the need for going to parties, without ever bothering to discuss it. I started driving, I continued to struggle with school, and I had totally given up on the Catholic Church, or any church for that matter.

I thought I was inexperienced at how to proceed with a normal relationship with the opposite sex, and I was determined to never mention my abuse by Whelan to my girlfriend or anybody else. I still carried on my shoulders a tremendous amount of guilt, and I felt like I was hiding my sick self from my girlfriend. I also had a problem with trusting her, or any other human being. It may have led to arguments, but the truth about my abuse would not come out. At times I felt as though the aftereffects of the abuse had disappeared and that I was evolving into a mature, unscathed human being. Then I would go to a party again and get bombed, and decide that I didn't want to be a responsible adolescent at all.

What for?

Being a responsible adolescent had never worked at school; why would it work on a Saturday night?

A main concern of mine at the time was how to handle my emotional involement with intimacy. The question in my mind was, "How does a teenage boy act with a girl, if he is ordinary and has not been molested?"

I didn't know. There were no instruction manuals I knew at the time to read that would teach me how to act as though I had not been sexually abused by a priest. I was unable to explain this, as I didn't understand it myself.

Nevertheless, I attempted to be the "normal boyfriend."

Our relationship was hectic, but we thought that we were madly in love with each other, at least on some days. On the days that we were not madly in love with each other, we really didn't know exactly what we were, or maybe we didn't know who we were. Flipping a coin each day to see who we would be that day would have been more productive and accurate.

I felt sometimes that I couldn't live without her, because I believed I had to have someone in my life at that time to make me think I was worth anything at all. The terrible insecurity of thinking that there was no such thing as religion, God, safety, or heaven was insurmountable.

My girlfriend gave me some kind of validation that I was desirable enough, at least to her, to keep on pushing.

Throughout the relationship, I struggled with feeling that I was living two lives. One was a normal teen life that included cars, movies, and days at the beach and a cute girlfriend I was very attracted to. The other life was that of a high school loser, hated by God and priests, who attracted weird sexual perverts and was destined for a future of countless failures. Eventually, I believed, the continued deception I was living would finally surface.

Somehow I managed to go out with my girlfriend for over a year without noticing if our relationship was a very good one or not. I still wasn't able to figure out what an "average" relationship should be like. It was too difficult

A Witch Wins JUSTICE

to lead a double life. But I felt I really wanted her and really cared for her.

One day, out of nowhere it seemed, she broke off our relationship, and I was crushed—more like devastated—but I had grown accustomed to surprises, confusion, and utter disappointment. So maybe I should have expected it. But it still felt as though a bomb had been dropped on me...again.

But the bigger bomb came shortly after.

I went to my best friend's house to cry on his shoulder and ask for advice. My girlfriend was there with him.

A double betrayal.

Was I ever in a daze. How could they both do this to me at once?

Just like Whelan and God, I thought. Another double betrayal.

Maybe all the betrayals in my life were meant to come in pairs.

I went back home to my dog Snoopy, the only creature on earth I could trust. As usual, Snoopy loved me back. It's no wonder many people say that they love dogs more than they love humans. Unconditional love is such a rare gift.

It was then in my senior year at Salesian that I truly realized my personality was significantly different than my happier, more successful years in grammar school. I didn't like whom I had turned out to be, and this notion became consuming. The nightmares continued, and my health was awkward. My classes were useless to me, and my interest in my future had dissolved. I was the deteriorating werewolf. At that time I had an English teacher named Brother Dan, whom I decidedly thought was peculiar. One unforgettable day, when I walked into English class, Bro. Dan was not there yet, but the whole class was. At the front of the class was his podium, and on it was his grade book, which was conveniently open. I walked up to the podium, and I was looking at the grade book, when a classmate sitting in front of the room asked me to tell him his grade. I did.

The next thing I knew, I felt a big pop in my ear, and I landed on the floor six feet away, unconscious. When I came to, seconds or minutes later I guess, some boys were gathering around me to pick me up. At this point I had no idea what had happened, and I felt as though I must have landed on the beach. I could feel the sand beneath me.

Now I remember. I used to hold a seashell against my ear, and I could hear the ocean. I could hear it now. It was wonderful. The seashell must have covered my ear; I couldn't hear the classroom noise at all. Sometimes you could taste the sand on the seashell too, and I tasted the sand now. It was on my tongue.

But as my foggy mind cleared, I realized It wasn't sand; it was worse.

A dirty linoleum school floor tastes terrible.

I felt the cold floor, and the dirt from it on my tongue. I must have opened my mouth when I landed. As I tried to spit out the filth I tasted, I noticed that the sound of the ocean in my ear was changing.

It started to ring instead, and the ocean disappeared. And there was no seashell. As the boys picked me up off the floor, I realized that Bro. Dan had punched me in the ear so hard, he knocked me out. Brother Dan was a

A Witch Wins JUSTICE

fairly large man, and I recall that at that time I still only weighed in at about one hundred ten pounds.

A few minutes later, I couldn't hear out of my ear, and I was carried down to an office room downstairs. There was blood in my ear, and I received no medical attention. The fact that a Salesian priest or brother would punch a student unconscious was not unheard of. What was more disturbing about the incident was that the Salesians faculty was so unconcerned with the injuries they inflicted on students. It was so common for a teacher to strike a student at the school that when an occurrence such as mine happened, the attitude of a lot of the boys would be one of complacency.

It might have occurred to me that the Salesian clergy was not very tolerant of me, which would have been obvious to most students in my position, but I chose to be oblivious.

I decided I dare not mention the incident to my parents, partly because of self-blame, and partly because I wanted to set all of my abuse aside and still try to act as though I was normal. It wasn't long after that incident that a friend of mine was at my house and made a comment in front of my father about Bro. Dan Riordan punching me out in class.

My father was shocked at first, then asked me why Bro. Dan would punch me like that. I told him what I had done, and my father felt that the punch was undeserved. But my father, being old-school Italian and very protective, had vindication in his mind, something I didn't anticipate at the time.

Salesian High School held a carnival-type celebration every year during the month of May, and accordingly,

After the Molester Disappeared

it was called the "Mayfest." Most Salesian students, their parents, the teachers, the clergy, and the supporters of the high school attended the function. It was usually a successful fundraiser, and there was food, games, and lots of publicity. Almost everybody I knew at the time went to the Mayfest that year, except me. I was depressed and apathetic. My mother went there to work and cook; my father went there to help. Or so I thought.

What I missed by not going to the Mayfest, in retrospect, I have had mixed emotions about. According to all my friends, many of whom were witness to the Mayfest "incident," my father was a man on a mission.

My father weaved through the Mayfest celebration, asking many of the clergy and several students where Bro. Dan was. When he was finally sent in the right direction, he approached Bro. Dan and verified who he was.

"Do you know Joey Piscitelli?" he further inquired.

"Yes," he said. "He's one of my English students."

"Well I'm his father," my dad said "And you're the guy who knocked him out in class, aren't you?"

Bro. Dan got defensive.

"Well Mr. Piscitelli, let me explain what happened."

Bro. Dan started to say something, witnesses say, when my father's fist connected with his jaw. Bro. Dan landed on the ground, his glasses broken and his face bloody. Instantly, bystanders pulled my father away. Brother Dan was immediately removed from the school and never seen again.

It finally became obvious to me that whenever a scandal occurred at Salesian, the priests and brothers involved would disappear. What I didn't think about at the time was this: where were they being sent?

A Witch Wins JUSTICE

Priests and brothers came and went at Salesian; no one really questioned why, or when—it didn't seem unusual. There was no publicity in those days in the media that revealed that one policy of the Catholic Church was to shuffle abusers from one school to another.

It was probably about this time that a new face appeared fitting the description well of what the students' whispering was all about. Although only innuendos at the onset, the boys quickly dubbed the new priest a "queer." I heard rumors that this priest had been at Salesians years before and was some sort of "homo" with young boys. His name was Fr. Dabbenne, and I cannot count how many times I heard him referred to as a "flaming" fruitcake. He had "hugged" me one time in the hallway, and I avoided him like the plague.

It was sometime after the Mayfest that Fr. Frank Vranjos, the school "counselor," removed me from class one day to tell me about a meeting. Since Fr. Frank was "Mr. Any Port in a Storm," to me, I was on guard about this "meeting."

He took me outside of the class and said, "Well, Joey, there's somebody I want you to meet. She's a very nice woman. I've known her for a while, and sometimes she goes to schools to talk to students. You'll like her."

I looked at him puzzled. "To talk about what?"

"Well, just talk about things, you know. She comes to talk to students who sometimes need someone to talk to."

He was very sketchy and evasive. I was suspicious.

"You'll like her," he repeated. "She's a counselor, and she wants to talk to you. She's from the Diocese of Oakland, and she goes to different schools in the Diocese to talk to kids about things."

I followed Fr. Frank to the office, and I walked into the office room to meet the counselor. She introduced herself, and added that she was a counselor sent by the Diocese of Oakland to talk to me—"about problems."

The counselor was a warm sort of person, probably around fifty years old. She dressed conservatively, and seemed professional, but was kind and receptive. She was on one side of a desk and asked me to sit down on the chair on the other side of the desk.

I did. She had a file in front of her, and she looked briskly through the file, and then at me.

"So tell me," she started, "is there anything you wanted to talk about?"

I looked at her bewildered.

"Are you having any problems in school that you need to talk to me about?" she repeated.

I looked at her carefully. It crossed my mind to proceed with caution.

"I don't know," I evaded.

"Well, let's see," she said calmly while looking at the file, "I noticed your grades have been dropping, and your performance at St. John's School when you were younger was better than it seems to be here. Your IQ tests were very high."

"Are you having any problems with your teachers?"

"Well, sort of," I answered carefully.

"What is it?" she asked too quickly.

"I guess I have a problem with the priests," I answered bravely.

There. I said it. Now, I wanted to go.

"What problem do you have with the priests?"

Her interest was really piqued. I got nervous. I was remembering the words of Whelan—"Nobody is going to believe your word against a priest." They were still stuck in my head.

"Well, they're weird," I responded carefully again.

I could see that she sensed something, and that she wasn't going to let it go so easily.

"What do you mean?" she quizzed.

I got a little braver.

"Well," I sort of cowered, "the priests are queer with the boys."

I immediately regretted it, and I was thinking of a way to change the subject at the first opportunity. But she persisted.

"What do you mean queer?" her voice changed a bit.

Now I had done it. There had got to be a way out, but I was torn between spilling my guts completely—letting it all out, or maybe just saying I was kidding or something, and leaving at once. She knew I was stalling.

"What do you mean the priests are queer?" She wouldn't let it go.

Where is this heading? I was thinking. What did I do now with my big mouth?

But I had to answer. I felt my face flush.

"You know," I blushed, "they're queer; they're weird."

It was all I could spit out. I didn't have the guts I thought I had. I had said enough, but I knew she got it this time. I didn't know the words "pedophile" or "child molester" yet, but even if I did, I would have been too scared to say them to her. But I was convinced she caught on finally.

After the Molester Disappeared

Her face showed her concern. It was as though she was sorry she heard me saying it.

"What priests are queer?" she asked after thinking a moment.

Boy, she's not going to stop there, I thought. This was very uncomfortable. I should not have opened this can of worms. I should have shut up. I sat there red-faced and ashamed.

She read me like a book. The uneasiness filled the room.

"You can tell me what's bothering you. I'm here to talk to you about your problems. Anything you tell me will be confidential, between the two of us."

She looked very caring, very concerned, and very honest. And I believed her.

"What priests are weird and queer?" she said calmly.

"Well," I courageously said, "Father Whelan, Brother Sal, and Father Dabbenne."

She didn't answer immediately. She picked up some files and looked through them for several minutes. Finally she looked back up at me. The suspense was driving me batty.

"Fr. Whelan and Bro. Sal Billante are no longer here," she said. "But Fr. Dabbenne is still here."

"Why do you think Fr. Dabbenne is queer?" She moved off of Whelan and Billante.

I was sorry she did that. Because they weren't there. It was easier to say something about the two who were missing, than the one who was still there, possibly in the next room.

"He's queer," I repeated.

I could see that she knew she was not going to get any details out of me, and she bounced around on subjects that I didn't even pay attention to, until I perked up when she asked about art.

I revealed to her that I wrote poems sometimes and doodled during class, and she seemed extremely interested. I had one of my "notebooks" with me. I mentioned to her that sometimes I drifted off in class and elsewhere, and that I drew cartoons, and wrote things that didn't make too much sense sometimes. I didn't realize at that time that this must have been a therapists dream: a journal of thoughts and pictures that a person who has problems has been keeping. She really wanted to see my notebook.

I had reservations about showing her the journal, mostly because it had some pictures that were graphic, and some dark poetry, and some pictures that I couldn't figure out myself. She kept asking to see the notebook.

I told her okay. She walked over to me gently and prompted me to show it to her. There was one particular picture that she seemed fascinated with. It was a picture of a boy in a straightjacket, being held up by puppet strings, and a priest was the puppeteer.

I thought her eyes were going to pop out of her head. She had a hard time containing herself, and her voice was excited. I didn't think the notebook was that fascinating.

"Joey," she began, "can I please take this notebook to show to just one person who is very close to me? No one else will see it, I promise you." She was pleading. I said yes, hoping that she was as honest and sincere as she purported to be.

After the Molester Disappeared

Drawing given to diocese therapist in 1972

A Witch Wins JUSTICE

Our meeting ended, and the counselor said she would see me in a week and would return the notebook then. I left the room with mixed emotions, not sure where all these new revelations would take me. I did know that I trusted her enough to give her my notebook and tell her my feelings about the priests. Finally, I thought, there was some kind of light at the end of the dark Salesian High tunnel.

But that light disappeared quickly. The next day, my mother came out from the school cafeteria where she worked, and caught me on the pavement between the school and the parking lot. She was visibly shaken, and crying.

"Joey," she said, "I need to talk to you."

"What's the matter?" I jumped, thinking something terrible had happened.

"Joey," she repeated, "what did you tell that lady?"

I was lost.

"What lady?" I said.

"The lady you talked to about school." She wiped her eyes.

"What did you tell that lady? Father Dabbenne is raving mad. I'm going to get fired from my job in the cafeteria, and you're going to get kicked out of school!"

She seemed hysterical, and I was stunned.

"Fr. Dabbenne says you told her that he was queer and that the priests are bad, and now you won't graduate."

My tongue was tied. I couldn't believe that the counselor had betrayed me like that.

I couldn't believe she told Dabbenne, and I couldn't believe he threatened to fire my mother from her job

After the Molester Disappeared

and kick me out of school. But there I was. The biggest mess of my life. How would I possibly fix this? I couldn't talk properly to answer my mother. Just burble came out of my mouth. She regained her composure and told me that I should go talk to Dabbenne and straighten things out as soon as possible.

That was just great. I would have to talk to Dabbenne, obviously to apologize, when I knew what he was, and when I knew what Whelan and Billante were. It just kept getting worse and worse.

But the saddest thing about it was that I had to make a decision then and there to preserve my mothers' job, and my diploma, by selling myself out mentally. I knew at this point that she would wait for me to explain what happened, but I elected to not tell her, because I anticipated that the Salesians would deny that anything had happened to cause this.

I left my mother there to believe that all that had happened was that I was mouthing off about Dabbenne. She did not know I was molested, and I did not want her to have the burden of that knowledge. I knew that the results of being outnumbered by several priests would be catastrophic. I was devastated. I had to go to face him, and bury my pride like the bloody underwear.

In 1972, there were no massive allegations of clergy abuse that rocked the media. I myself had never heard of any allegation at all. It would have been unthinkable at that time, and probably unbelievable, to accuse the priests of the wrongs that they were committing.

A dozen different thoughts went through my head in minutes. But the main concern was self-preservation. If the issue would boil down to who was lying, me, or several Salesian priests, I would risk not only taking myself down, but my mother as well.

I approached Dabbenne's office like a sick puppy that had just been beaten. And I knew I was in for another beating. But I went in anyway.

"Fr. Dabbenne," I started out stuttering, "can I talk to you?"

If looks could kill, as they say, he would have mutilated me and set me on fire.

"Why should I talk to you?" he yelled. "Do you know what you've done? You are going to get your mother fired, and yourself kicked out. How dare you talk about me to anyone."

"I'm sorry," I weakly responded.

"Sorry? You're sorry? Who do you think you are? I can ruin you, do you understand that?"

"Nobody will believe your word against a priest!"

My jaw dropped. Hearing those words put me back into Whelan's office. The exact words Whelan used. It was painfully eerie, beyond absorption. I thought I was going to float away again. I could do nothing else but stand there dumbfounded. Then I came to again. What could I possibly say now?

"How dare you talk about me," he started again. "It wasn't me, it was someone else!"

I think he surprised us both by saying that; it was almost some kind of slipped admission that he knew what was going on.

"You will be lucky if I let you continue here, do you understand that?" he continued screaming. "You'll be

After the Molester Disappeared

lucky if your mother stays, and you graduate; you'll be lucky if I let you."

He repeated threats and screams over and over again while the veins bulged at the side of his head. He was livid. Somehow, after continued apologies that seemed to go unnoticed, I left his office and walked away numb and whipped.

Fr. Bernard Dabbenne didn't kick me out. We both knew that my mouth would be zippered shut for the rest of my school term. But the Salesian nightmare didn't end there.

The priests had a way of talking to each other and covering for each other, as I was soon to find out, and the monster was bigger than I thought.

And Dabbenne had good reasons to be so disturbed by my talk to the counselor. I didn't know it at the time, but Dabbenne had been at Salesian High in the late 1950s and early 1960s. Salesian High School was a "seminary" in the 1950s. It was a school for boys who were studying to become priests. In 1961 a student had complained to the Salesian Provincial that Bernard Dabbenne had repeatedly molested him at the Salesian seminary.

That student later reported the molestation to the Richmond Police.

Dabbenne must not have wanted another complaint filed at Salesian for sexual abuse. But even more disturbing was the fact that the Salesians had complaints about Dabbenne several years before at the same school, but had sent him back there again. According to court testimony years later, the Salesians knowingly had sent Fr. Dabbenne and another serial molester named

A Witch Wins JUSTICE

Fr. Richard Presenti back to Salesian schools, after prior complaints of sexual molestation had been made.

It was shortly after the Dabbenne fiasco my senior year that I was asked to go see Fr. David Purdy, who was the director of the school. Fr. Purdy was a dark-haired man with stern features, someone I did not know well and who was not one of my teachers. He was an administrator. The only thing I personally knew about him was that he was present at the school dances and that he was known to "search" the boys as they entered the dances, to make sure that the boys "had no alcohol on them." Now this was ironic, because every time I went near Purdy, I thought he reeked of alcohol.

I arrived at Fr. Purdy's office, and he shut the door and told me to sit down. There was oddness in his demeanor, and I sat there quietly as he took his time thinking. His eyes were bloodshot, and I did not know if it was because he had just drank alcohol or if he had an allergic reaction to me, like most of the Salesian priests must have had.

He stared at me coldly and didn't speak for a couple of minutes, which added to the oddness of the meeting. He began to slowly circle around me, which was very agitating.

I couldn't help but think of Whelan and wonder if Purdy was going to attack me. If his intention was to build a scene of peculiarity and weirdness, he was succeeding.

Finally he began to speak in a soft monotone voice, adding to the utter creepiness of the meeting.

"Joey," he began, almost in a whisper, "you have a lot of problems."

After the Molester Disappeared

He stared at me hideously, as if he knew I was freaked out, and he seemed to me to be enjoying it.

"Nobody likes you," he continued ominously, "and you are very lonely."

As he spoke, I felt as though he was attempting to hypnotize me.

"People like you are always unhappy, and they eventually live a slow, horrible life and die a lonely death. I have seen people like you before, and I know that unhappy people like you are miserable inside, throughout their entire life, and there is only one way you can end that misery."

"There's only one way out for you. We both know what that is. It's suicide. We both know it's inevitable, he repeated. Suicide is the only answer."

Purdy calmly and methodically repeated these words over and over again, as he circled slowly around me, stopping every few moments to stare intently at me. His hands were cupped, as though he was conducting a sermon and had rehearsed the script for maximum effect.

He relentlessly continued the morbid sermon and repeatedly told me that "suicide is the only answer."

He was enjoying it, and now I know he was getting off on it. It was stimulating for him to think he could hypnotize a person into the act of suicide.

How powerful it must have felt. Maybe it was just like molestation, and the reward was the ecstasy of complete domination over a victim.

Eventually his words began to muffle into an inaudible sound, and I looked away from him.

A Witch Wins JUSTICE

I stared at the picture of Saint Don Bosco, the founder of Salesians, on his wall. I thought Bosco was a spineless bastard to let Purdy continue the suicide talk. There was a statue of Don Bosco outside the school, in the yard. The statue also must have been a spineless bastard. I turned to look out the window and slowly felt myself drift toward it. Then I passed through it, and I began to float outside the window and up above the trees outside, and I passed through the clouds, and I entered the chamber, where the inquisitors were talking to the witches on trial. They were cold and methodical too, and they too had bloodshot eyes like Purdy's. The inquisitors also spoke in a monotone voice, fascinated by the thought of death, as though it was sexually stimulating for them.

Perhaps it was for Purdy also, to speak of taking your life as though it was expected; but the inquisitors' anticipation of certain death, which they delightedly held over a victim's head, was always brought to fruition, and the vulnerability of the victim was a prize they were addicted to, a sickness that must have been constantly fed and replaced. I hovered over the witch they were torturing and knew there was nothing I could do to change the inevitable outcome; there will always be Purdys, in the past, and in the future.

I left the chamber, and felt selfish for abandoning the helpless witch who was still there on trial, being spoken to in a soft monotone Purdy voice, hearing about her impending death. I saw that film of death covering her blank eyes, and I knew it was too late. I shamefully left her there to expire.

When I floated back to Salesian school, I passed by the statue of the spineless Don Bosco and told him what a bastard I thought he was, and how painful it was to see Purdy talk kids into suicide.

Bosco said nothing and closed his eyes. He knew. What a coward.

He was ashamed, but that was no consolation.

I returned to Purdy's office, entering through the window; he hadn't noticed I had left. He was still talking about suicide, his bloodshot eyes intact, perhaps needing to be soothed by a shot of whiskey. I got up out of my chair and asked him if he was finished, and he stared at me in bewilderment. Possibly he was wondering if he was successful with his suggestion.

He repeated himself one last time.

"Suicide is the only answer."

I emerged from his office in a stupor. It was as if the Salesian priests were having some sort of contest to see who could torture me the best. The director of the school just called me into his office to talk me into suicide. I didn't think any priest was going to top this latest testament to absolute horror at a Catholic school.

Fr. Purdy's suicide talk was what blunt psychologists call a "**mind fuck.**"

There's no better definition of it. Purdy wasn't going off the handle in a rage, or having an angry outburst at the spur of the moment. It was a cold, calculated attempt by an adult to persuade a teenager into taking his life. How a supposed "man of God" could even think of such an act is inconceivable. I got in my car when I left school that day, and turned on the radio. The sound that came out of the speaker was Purdy. He kept saying the same thing over, and over again.

"Suicide is the only answer. Suicide is the only answer."

A Witch Wins JUSTICE

I had to turn the radio off; the sound coming out of it reeked of alcohol. The alcohol was spilling out of the speaker and onto the floor.

A few days later, the Diocese therapist returned. I went to see her for the follow-up, and not one word was mentioned about the last meeting's talk about Dabbenne, Whelan, or Bro. Sal Billante. I found this fact peculiar, as the issue was foremost on her mind when we had met last. This led me to believe logically that she must have had contact with Dabbenne and the gang, and they must have told her that the "mess" was cleared up and to move on. I told her that Fr. Purdy had tried to talk me into suicide, and she almost fainted. She calmly told me that she thought it was terrible, and that she hoped I didn't take him seriously. I never heard from her again. I am sure that Purdy denied it.

The Salesian "Code of Silence" was now in effect. I didn't mention it to anyone else, and I wondered if Purdy had ever said those stupid, insensitive things about suicide to any other students. There have been several students who had attended Salesian who did commit suicide, and I can't help but wonder if any of them have had the misfortune of having Purdy give them his disturbing talk, and if he in fact was the cause of their fatal decision.

My mother continued to work at the school cafeteria, and she cooked dinner for the priests in the evenings before she went home. My brother worked in the evenings serving the priests their dinner, which was actually in a private, separate dining room attached to the cafeteria. He also cleaned up the dining room and tables after their dinner, then washed dishes and went home.

After the Molester Disappeared

On some occasions, when he was unable to be there, he would have a substitute take his place. On very few occasions, when his substitute could not make it, he would ask me to fill in for him—a task I avoided as much as possible.

On one of those unfortunate days that he had me substitute for him, I had to wait on and serve the dining room full of Salesian priests, which was a dreadful experience. When I first entered the room with their food, the entire room fell silent. During the second entrance I made, when I brought their drinks, they kept silent until I left the room, and then began to talk.

I overheard Fr. Presenti, the administrator, say to the others,

"Who told that son-of-a-bitch to take his brother's place? I sure the hell don't want that big mouth in here."

Fr. Presenti had strong reason to not want my big mouth around the priests for sure.

Prior to his placement at another Salesian High, a molestation victim had reported him to Salesian officials, and the Salesians had typically promised that Presenti would not be placed around children again. But there he was at a high school again with access to students. After the dinner, Presenti came into the back kitchen and told me that I did a terrible job and that he did not want me to return to substitute for my brother again. I was actually in agreement with the deplorable priest. I did not want to return to the Salesian dining room again ever, and I couldn't bear to be in the same room with even one of them.

By 1973 I had given up on trying to bring my grades up to par. I was too far behind. I just hoped I would be

A Witch Wins JUSTICE

able to graduate; my head was so stuffed with nightmares, headaches, and confusion that I wanted to jump out of my skin.

But the Salesian poison was still flowing.

Toward the end of my senior year, I was in the second-floor hallway, walking with two friends toward my class, and there were other classes going on. The classroom doors, which were opaque glass, were closed, and you cannot see through them clearly, like bathroom-window glass. I was about two feet away from a closed classroom door, and my friend pushed me into the door to be funny then ran down the hall. The priest who was teaching the class, Fr. Al Mengon, opened the door and saw me.

"Piscitelli," he yelled, "come over here now. Why are you trying to disrupt my class?"

"I'm not," I answered, "I was pushed."

By now, the friend who had pushed me was not in sight. Fr. Mengon shut the door to his classroom, and he was in the hallway with me all alone.

"I don't like you," he said, "and none of the other priests do either. You're a smartass, and you've got a big mouth."

I knew he was referring to me having a big mouth because of the issues with the scandal concerning Dabbenne, Whelan, Billante, and now Purdy, and this had nothing to do with the bump on the door. I motioned to leave, and he stopped me.

"Stand still," he commanded.

"What?" I said, puzzled.

He grabbed both my arms by my shoulders, with both of his hands, and said again, "Stand straight and still."

After the Molester Disappeared

I was confused as to why he apparently wanted me to stand so still, but I found out.

Mengon looked sternly into my eyes; and then swiftly and firmly kneed me directly in the groin. I never expected it at all, and stood there straight and took the full force of his powerful knee without any defense or flinch whatsoever. It was much worse than when Bro. Dan punched me in the ear and knocked me out.

I went down like I had been hit by a truck. I couldn't catch my breath; I couldn't even groan. I opened my mouth and no sound came out, and for a few seconds I thought my heart had even stopped. I realized my face was on the floor after about a minute, and looked up to see him pointing down the Hall.

"Now get out of here," he snarled, grinding his teeth, "and don't you dare bother my class again. You're lucky I don't have you suspended."

I firmly believed at that point, that when you die and go to hell, it must be staffed by Salesian priests. I also wondered if it was at all possible, while I lay there in pain, if I would ever be capable of producing children in the future.

I closed my eyes, and I was all alone, my face glued to the floor. I could see directly straight down the long hallway floor, and it looked like it was rippled. Floors aren't always perfectly straight, I thought, and this one was an example of an old floor that had seen its days of aging. I remembered that as a child whenever I was lying on the wood floor, the floor would look warped and rippled when I laid my head on it and stared down the hall. How odd it was to me. Because when you stand up looking at the floor, it seems to be perfectly even.

A Witch Wins JUSTICE

It was comparable to life: how we perceive perfection, or make assumptions that people are honest and straightforward; and in actuality, up very close and in detail, we see how warped and imperfect they really are, just like the floor. The more I stared at the floor, the more I seemed to rise up above it. I left my body there on the floor, and stared at it pitifully.

I thought it best to let it rest for a while—I was sure that Fr. Al had done some damage to it. What a loser body it was, laying there immobile.

It was time to go outside the window again. It was conveniently high above the ground already, and I flew out and up toward the third-floor window. As I looked through the window into the third-floor multipurpose room, I saw the shadows of the figures of Whelan and God molesting a young boy in the room. It was exactly where they had molested me, and the boy they were violating looked exactly like I did.

They had a canvas in the room, and they were taking turns splattering blood across it, but much of the blood splatter hit the window I was looking through, and it began to gather on the window and roll down the glass. I watched as I hovered outside looking through the window; the blood rolling down made the glass look striped. Each red stripe looked like the red stripe on my underwear, the underwear I had thrown over the fence several months back.

All of a sudden, God looked out the window and saw me staring at the scene. He was pissed, I could tell. He thought that he and Whelan were alone. He vindictively held up my bloody underwear and waved it at me.

I knew it.

After the Molester Disappeared

God had gone back and retrieved the bloody underwear I had thrown over the fence that day in my backyard, and he had saved it. He had also saved the rock I had wrapped the underwear around that day to make it sail over the fence. God threw the rock at me, and I flew out of the way. The rock went through the third-floor multipurpose room window, shattering it, and went sailing onto the ground. I left the window and went back to my painful body lying on the hallway floor. I decided to finally get up.

After I had collected myself, I limped down the hallway and left school.

I considered telling my father, but I was closer to graduating now, and I decided not to go through another scandal, more threats, and who knows what else the Salesian School of Horrors would have in store for me. It was useless.

The next day, I was on the school grounds in the back of the school, and I looked up at the third floor. There were two men fixing a broken window of the multipurpose room. There was glass on the ground, and the janitor was cleaning it up. I walked over to the janitor, and I asked what had happened.

"Someone must have broken the window," he answered. "They must have got cut pretty bad—there was blood all over the broken pieces of glass."

Just then, Fr. Al Mengon walked past me on the ground. He laughed when he saw me, and he winked at me in contempt. It wasn't till years later I was told that Fr. Al Mengon had been accused of abuse also. At the same time, my mother told me that Mengon had abused a girl in the school library. He was later shipped by the Salesians to the continent of Africa.

A Witch Wins JUSTICE

By the time I graduated from the school, I had been molested several times, had been attacked, had been raped, had my eardrum busted, had been betrayed by the therapist, had been threatened by the principal to keep quiet or get kicked out of school, had an administrator try to talk me into suicide, and had been severely damaged in the groin.

I graduated in the summer of 1973 on the fumes of what credits I accumulated when I was actually mentally present at school, which was remarkable; I did not think that my mind was operating at even half capacity. Leaving Salesians was to me comparable to being released from hard prison. What a letdown from my original plans when I first arrived at that school. I felt like I was truly leftover "Catholic Garbage."

But graduation from that institution was much more than an adolescent wake up call. I had to face the realization that my prior four years of high school, which should have been preparation for college and a productive adult life, were gone completely.

The relief of graduating from that school, combined with the realization that I could recapture those irreparable years, was a bitter mix.

But even more detestable was the disingenuous Catholic High School graduation ceremony, presented by the Salesian institution that harbored so many accused child molesters.

How many students present at the time who were concealing their horrific experiences brought upon them by the nest of clerical child abusers, I will never know. Years later I would meet several of the victims, but at

After the Molester Disappeared

the time I was still unaware of the devastation that was wrought by some of the perpetrators that had administrated the Salesian establishment.

Having the spirituality I was raised with shattered by an egregious molester was insurmountable. Not only was I unable to face the fact that all concepts of God that were implanted in my psyche literally since birth were completely destroyed, but my resultant warped image of what should really be spirituality was annihilated.

I left the school feeling worthless, cheated, and victimized. I really did not know where to go from this point, and my self-image was a deterrent from progression into manhood. The thought of sharing my experiences with someone who would understand me or help me was inconceivable. What I really wanted to do was to become a new person and take back the last four years of hell, and relive my life again as a normal student. I would gladly welcome the illusion that I could have a fresh new start, but I knew better. And I am still surprised, at this time in my life, that I did not become a drug addict, because the desire to leave this planet was overwhelming. But I decided to take a different path; those stars I encountered as a child may have induced my determination to explore what life still had to offer me; and that may have been my saving redemption when I was seventeen.

Collecting Books and Learning

Shortly after leaving the Salesian School of Horrors, I began my journey to the post-high school world. I would attempt to leave the abuse by the hands of the unremorseful molesting priest behind, as if that was possible, and "get over it."

I began to collect books. That was thirty-nine years ago. I had no plan to speak of. I just wanted to search for some spirituality. Many Psychologists say that there is an area of your brain that prompts an inclination to seek spirituality, and I had a yearning for something that I knew was missing. I did not know exactly what it was, but I was inclined to keep searching. I could not explain my propensity for this spirituality, especially after what had happened to me at school, but the inclination was strong. I wasn't positive why, but I felt an intense desire to investigate witches, witchcraft, and paganism.

I did not have full realization at the time that this desire might have been instigated by the fact that I was a reincarnated witch, but I had an inkling.

I began to read as much as possible about any and all "occult" beliefs and was surprised at what I had learned. All religions before the "birth of Christ" were Pagan. The early pagans were not devil worshipers, nor did they believe in Satan, which was actually a Christian invention. The early "witches" were, in fact, "wise women" and "wise men" who had passed along

A Witch Wins JUSTICE

knowledge of herbs and medicines for centuries, and who were eventually made scapegoats by Catholics and Christians as organized religion became a political power. The Church had covered over most Pagan holidays with new Christian holidays and branded pagans and witches as Satan worshipers. This resulted eventually in the killing, raping, and torturing of tens of thousands of mostly innocent young girls and women at the direction of the Catholic Church, who wanted to establish itself as the one true religion.

I felt mysteriously all too familiar with the pain of the witch burnings. Some say it was the result of my being abused by the Catholic Church, and the transferring of the psychological similarity of the sex abuse I endured to the abuse of witches by the same Church. It is an interesting theory, but my first nightmares of being burned outside the church were eleven years before the priest molested me, and before I had ever heard of witches.

When I first read about the witch burnings and the Inquisition, I could hardly function. I had more nightmares, similar to those I had as a very young child, which felt more like horrible memories than nightmares. The reading of the first few books I acquired concerning the witch tortures and burnings was so incredibly familiar to me that I was certain I was there. The dreams of early childhood were being bumped back to the surface. I was beside myself with anxiety, and I could not conceive how an organized religion like the Catholic Church would instigate and condone such an inhuman horror.

The books I read also brought back the surrealistic experiences that had occurred when I was molested, and the flashbacks of the chamber, and the trials I had seen during those abusive experiences. It all began to blend together. How could God have allowed this cruelty, which was done in his name?

The memories of what had happened at Salesian school would haunt me many nights in vivid recollections. But the additions of the witch trials and tortures were becoming more intense and graphically precise, to the point that I became clearly convinced of my reincarnation, the proof of which had started when I was two or three. I was disappointed that I did not have the capacity to understand it at that age, and my mother had suffered so many nights and days in my early years wondering what was wrong with my strange dreams. I certainly did not want to explain it to her now, as it felt as though it would be totally unproductive and possibly would frighten her even more. One of the things I learned from my investigation into the witch tortures and atrocities was that when "witches," or those accused as witches, were sent to trial, they nearly always lost the trials and were sentenced to torture and death. Little did I know at that time when I first read these books as a young teen, that I would be in a court jury trial against the clergy of the Catholic church thirty-five years later myself.

It was shortly after I started collecting and reading these books in the 1970s that I came across a few books that mentioned witchcraft in Italy. I thought it was interesting that the Italian Witches, the *Strega*, had beliefs that were similar to those of my mother. I knew that my family was Catholic, but some of the verbiage and practices of my grandparents and parents were mixed with *Stregheria*, which was the term for Italian Witchcraft. There

A Witch Wins JUSTICE

was mentioning of *malochio*, which was "the evil eye"; and *Befana*, which was the *Strega's* celebration of the Winter Solstice. And there other beliefs and "superstitions" that had been handed down and actually blended with Catholicism somehow in my family. I recalled the mixed traditions, the altars, the confusing explanations, and the questions I had eventually abandoned in my past that had never been answered satisfactorily.

Of particular interest was reading about the worship of Diana in Italy. It rang a bell. I recalled that years before, my mother had mentioned that the altars she remembered as a child had been made in honor of Diana, whom my mother had thought might have been Mary the Mother of God.

Diana, as I mentioned earlier, was the Queen of Witches in Italy. But it was very rewarding to see that the Italian heritage pieces were starting to fit together and that I could make at least a little bit of sense out of the confusion concerning the Italian Craft. I wished I had been fortunate enough to be handed down some tradition, or some explanation, or anything at all concerning the Witches of Naples or Italy.

I made my first "Pagan" altar in my bedroom when I was fourteen. My mother was shocked at first, but she calmed down a few days afterwards.

She said later that "it looked like something Grandma would have made."

Why I made the altar and where I got the ideas for it were a mystery to me at the time, but it came from somewhere, and I was amazed at how I had automatically constructed an altar from a fog of a memory. Or was it a memory? I really didn't know.

Collecting Books and Learning

The main thing to me was that it was there in my room and I had made it myself, but it was "too weird" to my brothers, sisters, and friends. The books I collected were strange to them also. Nevertheless, I continued for years to collect books on Paganism and the Craft, and I have never stopped.

I became a Pagan Witch in 1981, and I developed my own understanding of what I considered my Path to be. I practiced witchcraft and magick, and I kept developing ideas and tenets through the years, as a result of what I had learned in the books and what I had experienced from my practice of the Craft. And my thirst for knowledge of witchcraft and magick kept increasing. It was much more spiritual to me than anything I had ever learned from the twisted nest of molesters at Salesian High.

I bought and acquired books on mysticism, occultism, Witches, Witchcraft, Magick, Buddhism, reincarnation, astral projection, Shamanism, reclaiming, goddesses, gods, Wicca, La Vechia Religione, Stregheria, Tarot, Paganism, Sorcery, Cabala, high Magick, low Magick, ceremonial Magick, relativity, electromagnetic fields, and more.

I also bought books and writings by Albert Einstein, James Maxwell, Nicola Tesla and Isaac Newton. I had a particular interest in books that were concerned with atomic theory and the theories of space and time, and their correlations with Magick.

The collection just grew and grew. I have books that are three hundred years old and books that are one month old. I have acquired over two thousand books, and I have tried to read them all completely in the last forty years.

A Witch Wins JUSTICE

By digesting the books and accumulating knowledge of magick, I began to piece my life together. It became clear to me that I was predestined to learn about my past life and educate myself for a reason.

I came to believe that one of the main reasons why magick would not work for some people, besides the lack of sincerity and intent, was the fact that most people had been trained as humans to be confined to the laws of linear time and thus were unable to "travel" to manipulate energy. Many books brushed the surface of this concept. Some of those books referred to the "travel" as astral travel or traveling to another plane, but they did not describe the travel as being connected to the theory of relativity or of light, or the absence of time.

Many books on witchcraft and magick, when describing magick, discussed the "drawing of energy" and the sources for energy—such as personal power, divinity, kundalini, or the power from the earth—but did not drag relativity into the pages that I can recall. This eluded me, but it did not matter, as the important things they had written were concerning the use of that energy in magick, and the Magickian's ability to "transfer" that energy elsewhere or use it somehow.

I was most fascinated with Karma, and the belief in reincarnation. At this point in my life, especially after all I had been through, including my experiences with my earliest dreams as a child, it was evident who I was in the past. It was also evident how I traveled to other places in time and space, and it seemed clear to me I was here to see and do everything for a reason.

Even the book collecting was predestined. Nothing was coincidence. There was a Karmic reason I had collected

Collecting Books and Learning

books, to ingest knowledge for a place in linear time I had not reached yet. I still did not know what that was, but I was certain that there was an imperative reason.

After I had been molested, I had never considered the possibility that I would someday get justice for what the church had done to me.

In any life.

I was uneducated about options, what had occurred, and what I was capable of doing in the future. I went about my life, working, stumbling, and suffering many times from the side effects of the abuse. The effects were like that of a psychological and emotional roller coaster. Sometimes victims of abuse are able to bury the trauma for years and not deal with it. Many times the side effects of abuse are not directly linked to child abuse, unless pointed out by professionals.

I tried to sidestep my abuse by heading in different directions. I still kept reading and collecting the Pagan-based books, and I did not consciously plan any retribution for anyone.

I avoided the church adamantly. I married in 1979 to a beautiful woman who I thought could possibly have also been an abused witch in an earlier life, who also avoided the Catholic Church. She was raised by an Italian Grandmother, who also mixed *Stregheria* with Catholicism and did not realize it.

Talk about destiny.

I became a contractor about thirty years ago, and I primarily built and remodeled houses for a living. When the roller coaster dipped down, I was depressed and anxious, and I would have to lift myself out of the drop by practicing my own eclectic magick.

A Witch Wins JUSTICE

I began to meet and contact other pagans and witches about twenty-five years ago, and I slowly entered some hidden circles of social and magickal activity. I did not share this information at that time with my Catholic relatives, or working contacts, as I considered it private and felt as though it would lead to intimidation. My parents obviously noticed I had never gone back to church since high school, and my close friends thought that some of my activities and beliefs were "a little odd." But oddness was acceptable to me.

I built a Pagan altar in my home about 1982, and that probably was the incident that prompted my family and acquaintances to question who and what I really was. The altar contained candles, crystals, pagan symbols, and a variety of items I had collected through the years. By that time of course, it did not matter. I began to notice at that period that magick seemed to work for me, because when I was very intent on doing a project or finding a building that needed remodeling or a similar task, I always managed to do it, irrespective of the forces against me.

It also occurred to me at that time in my life that when I really concentrated on channeling my will with intent, it usually worked—the further results of the art of "magick."

My real curse in life, which kept recycling, was the "downtime," which I attribute to the fallout from the clergy abuse. It kept coming back to bite me.

I finally consulted a lawyer about 20 years ago or so, to ask if there was anything I could do to seek retribution and justice for being molested at Salesian High School by the abusive priest. He told me that the statute of limitation had passed and that I had no legal recourse.

Collecting Books and Learning

Irrespective of this advice, I sensed an odd feeling at the time, that something was occurring in the "energy" in the universe. I had been reading books about relativity and electromagnetic properties, and I started to slowly incorporate the scientific properties with my magickal practice, with peculiar results.

Probably the most important book I read concerning the practice of Magick was *La Madre della Magia—Dea di Energia* (*The Mother of Magick—Goddess of Energy*) by Strega Viola.

This particular definition struck me:

The Mother of Magick is a deity that is a cosmic form of energy, an energy that consists of the interconnection of the entire universe. Since the entire universe, including all living things, is made of energy, which can be broken down into atomic particles, the Magickal deity is part and parcel of all matter in the entire cosmos.

The deity can be invoked with any religion, or science. The deity IS all religion, and all science. The deity, in effect, is consistent with the absence of time and the interconnection of all energy forms, existing before and after death, irrespective of scientific or religious boundaries.

The more I understood the Mother of Magick, the more I understood cause and effect, and the more I understood Karma, and the Magick Craft itself.

I was aware that most people I knew considered the practice of Magick very strange, and I think they may have considered it delusional. I have heard it said that some clergy abuse victims seek Pagan paths specifically because they were hurt by a person that represents the church, and that the victim associates the church with historic evil, out of confusion and misinterpretation of the damage that was done to them.

That may be accurate in some cases, and rightfully so. But I did my homework, and investigated and read considerably. There lies the difference between being disillusioned by a trauma, as opposed to logically considering the consequences and rationally making an informed decision. I kept collecting and reading.

I was aware that I had fallen from the church because of a clergy molester, so I did research myself to discover what had happened, why it happened, and what were the alternatives. And I was satisfied with what I was learning, that there was in fact a legitimate historic reason why I had an aversion to the Church.

Everything I did, or read, spelled Karma.

I began to attend different Pagan gatherings about that same time, and I enjoyed the enthusiasm and dedication of the witches I had met. They all seemed genuine, very spiritual, and respectful of nature and all living things. Most importantly, I think they all had chosen the Pagan path because they wanted to, and not because it was chosen for them by parents or forced upon them by anyone.

I do not know any witches who attend gatherings or meetings that go there to avoid burning in hell as a punishment. I have never met a witch or magickian who believes in hell or Satan. Nearly all of the witches and pagans I know are genuinely drawn to the path, and intentionally chose their direction after personal consideration and investigation.

Collecting Books and Learning

A pagan friend of mine suggested a theory years ago that perhaps I learned and practiced the art of magick because subconsciously, and on a different plane in the universe, I was aware that some day I may have the opportunity to seek justice, and I would need the power of magick to use against the evil powers of the opposition from the Church hierarchy who protected their molesters.

Interesting; again it spelled Karma.

I continued to practice magick and witchcraft, and it became second nature, or perhaps it should be called first nature. My wife and I had two children, and I did not want them to go to Catholic school as I did, because I was so mistrusting of the church. I also never brought my children to church; however, I gave them the option of going to any place of worship they chose, but I would not choose it for them.

I started "The Coven of the Purple Witch" in 1988. Several local witch friends I had met gathered occasionally for pagan practices for many years. I wrote many of my own rituals, and I continued to participate in gatherings of other groups as well. I wrote spells and rituals to "counter" the evils of the Church clergy responsible for child molestation, and for Church hierarchy cover-ups of the crimes, and I still had no tangible knowledge of any opportunity that would arise in the future to seek justice for the crimes committed against me by the Church.

I practiced the art of trying to communicate with my unconscious to access the untapped "energy" we are all made of.

I became increasingly aware of the power of blending magick, timelessness, and ritual, and how the use

A Witch Wins JUSTICE

of symbolism aided to manipulate energy with will. But I did not know when I would ever use this knowledge to seek justice. I felt an odd transformation was occurring, and although I did not understand it, I sensed that something was happening that would affect a change in the future. It was as if I was practicing and storing an unused potential, waiting for the Karma and opportunity to tap me on the shoulder.

Sometimes I would meditate or trance to travel backward toward the burning times, or attempt regression to see myself in the past, and it was very difficult. Other times I entered the past world with ease, aware that the absence of time was the key to the manipulation of energy. I began to feel more and more familiar with the witch trials, and more and more familiar with the sense of impending justice lingering in the universe; I just could not grasp it, yet.

> *My solution was to analyze the concept of time. Time cannot be absolutely defined...*
> —ALBERT EINSTEIN

I joined a group called SNAP in 2002. SNAP is The Survivors Network of those Abused by Priests. I became a leader in the Bay Area for SNAP shortly afterwards. I did not mention my paganism to the members of SNAP at events or protests, or at support group meetings with survivors, as I felt my religious preference was not an issue for discussion when protesting against molesters—it was irrelevant. I donated hundreds of hours to aid others in healing and recovering from clergy abuse.

Collecting Books and Learning

The SNAP Organization is nondenominational and accepts all people of all beliefs, Christian or not, and has no opinion of the religious preferences of its members. It is truly a neutral organization.

During the period from 2002 through 2009, I protested all over the state of California against clergy abusers of the Catholic Church and other churches as well. I participated in hundreds of protests and press events, and I was responsible for the removal of several priests from their positions, and some from ministry altogether. I personally fought a vehement battle with Cardinal William Levada, and I wrote several letters to Cardinal Ratzinger, the former head of the Catholic "Congregation of the Doctrine of the Faith." I wrote dozens of letters to the Pope and the Cardinals, and the Bishops of the Bay Area.

In keeping with their true natures, they showed no respect or decency by failing to respond at all.

I continued to send them countless letters denouncing their crimes and cover-ups of sexual abuse of innocent children, and they failed to display any response or accountability.

I realized this made them livid, and I didn't care.

Again, it was destiny.

Reconstructing my Reincarnation

To attempt the reconstruction of my past life as a tortured Witch, I accumulated numerous books on reincarnation, past life retrieval, and other similar topics. I combined the knowledge I had gained from these books and blended that information with what I had gathered from my many books on magick and witchcraft, and I came to my own conclusions. The main contributor for the foundation in my belief in reincarnation was the fact that I had the memories and experiences as a two- and three-year-old child that contained the "videos" in my head of my former life as a persecuted witch.

That I was unable to decipher them when I remembered them as a toddler is insignificant. What is significant is that I did have the dreams and memories of being tortured, and burned at the stake, without an outside influence or suggestion by anyone or anything at the time; and I was advanced at such an early age to communicate the stories; and my IQ was intact considerably as a toddler. I walked at six months old and talked well before I was two years old. That head start at such an early age was a significant advantage toward retrieval of the fuzzy memories of a past life, which a lot of people lose early in childhood, making their retrieval of past lives very difficult.

The additional discoveries that I made concerning my relationships with past memories and timelessness, and the ability to connect to hidden memories that had similarities to trauma, trance, and meditation, were certainly critical. The most important fact I observed was this:

> *Not only can the effect of trauma hide memories of the past, it can also bring back memories of the distant past to the forefront.*

Or, in other terms, I believe further that trauma, meditation, trance, and magick can induce recollection of collective memories, and scenes from lifetime(s) that can be retrieved, but not necessarily in chronological order.

One of the most perplexing views on reincarnation that I have come across is the view by many organized religions, including the Roman Catholic religion, that reincarnation "does not exist." Yet those same organizations preach and teach about "life after death."

Apparently, after you die, according to these religions, you go to heaven with God, and you spend that time eternally with him in glory and splendor. Or if you were a "bad" guy, for example, you go to hell and burn forever with Satan. But where were you before you were born? Nowhere, from what I can gather from these organizations.

It is also important to note that the Catholic Church accepted the belief in reincarnation hundreds of years ago, and then changed its views and acceptance of this belief somewhere about the third century.

So in effect, the Church changed from accepting reincarnation to accepting the belief in "half of reincarnation."

To me this was absurd. I find it impossible to believe you can go somewhere after you die if you weren't anywhere before you were born.

It's both, or nothing.

The Harris Poll of 2003 states that 27 percent of people in the United States believe in reincarnation. The poll also states that 80 percent of people believe in "half of reincarnation"—that is, the belief that they will die and go to heaven afterwards with God.

What happens when you reincarnate?

I would revert to the Magickal Jewish Cabala for some interesting information at this point. The Cabala basically states that at the top of the "Tree of Life" is endless light, and nothingness. In my own opinion, that translates as unseen, yet pure and powerful energy. We are all made of energy, and when we pass on, we revert back to energy.

In addition, I add that if you die, and reach "God" or divinity— whoever or whatever you believe that is—you achieve that pure energy form. "Clock time" stops, and you are energy particles—like electrons: assumed to be there, yet invisible. Your energy is in existence as something that appears to be "nothing." Matter and energy cannot be created or destroyed; they can only change.

Or move to another place.

And beyond death and beyond birth, there is no existence of "time"; it is not relevant.

We exist in this timeless realm between incarnations.

Many witches and magickians, and some Christians I know for that matter, believe that when you die, you do enter the universe as energy, and that this energy is also "what God is." Some say that we are all "God" and all part of the universal "God" as shared energy.

A Witch Wins JUSTICE

This is not a "God" in the true Christian sense; this is a cosmic belief. We are all connected, and we all share energy with the universe.

I believe Einstein was correct about cosmic religion: we are all connected—by energy and the universe, and we know little about the secrets that exist beyond life.

In addition, I also believe that when you die, your energy form does not enter back into your "human self" until your next birth. The human body is just a vehicle for that energy. That energy is part and parcel of your "soul." So in effect, we change shape or form into shared energy after we die, and we reenter the world again and repeat the cycle.

I needed to discover where I came from and why my life was what it was, why the things that happened to me during my youth had occurred, and if I had been predestined for a lesson in this life. Timelessness, matter, and energy are truly related.

Energy, that can be transformed into human thought, which existed once in the universe, is part and parcel of the complicated process of reincarnation.

We are sometimes reincarnated to perform "unfinished business" in our "life," to learn lessons, and I certainly believe that the Church had unjustly "convicted" me in a trial in a past life.

I further believe that my "mission" in this life was to correct a wrong, to gain more knowledge of the Pagan Craft, to beat the church in a court jury trial for child sex abuse, and to be an advocate for other sexual abuse victims of the church or clergy. It was no coincidence that I was tortured and burned at the stake as a witch by the Church, I was able to remember it as a child, I was victimized by the church as an adolescent, and I became a witch again.

It was predestined for me to discover my identity as a witch, to practice the art of magick, and to seek justice from the hierarchy of the church in this incarnation, as the law of cause and effect, and Karma would dictate.

And so it happened that way, because it was supposed to.

Again, there are no coincidences.

I assert that the cosmic religious experience is the strongest and the noblest driving force behind scientific research.

—ALBERT EINSTEIN

Into the Millennium

In the year 2003, the State of California created a law that enabled victims of child sexual abuse to sue "the organizations" responsible for minors abused in the past by employees of those organizations.

The law temporarily lifted the statute of limitations to sue an organization in a civil case, not a criminal case, no matter when the abuse occurred; this meant a victim of abuse could sue an organization that was negligent for abuse that happened decades ago. In order to successfully sue the organization, a victim had to be under the age of eighteen when the abuse occurred, and the organization had to have knowledge that the victim was in danger by the molester before the molester committed the act.

In other words, the organization had to have prior knowledge that the abuser was a threat, either because of a former complaint, or because the organization knew, or should have known, that the abuser might do it again. The organization had to be negligent and knowingly put the child at potential risk. The organization did not have to be a church. Unfortunately for the Catholic Church—which had been riddled with thousands of

A Witch Wins JUSTICE

sexual molesters for at least the last hundred years, had known and covered up countless sex crimes against children, and had knowingly transferred egregious sex offenders intentionally, it was inevitable that most of the lawsuits would be filed against the Roman Catholic Church.

I was sleeping, in the year 2002, when I had a dream that the Magick law of Karma had recycled through time, and that I was about to enter the period of my life when I would approach that predestined occurrence. The California law was part of that Karmic destiny.

I filed a lawsuit against the Catholic Church, the Salesians Catholic Order of Priests, and the Diocese of Oakland in 2003 for being molested as a minor by Fr. Steve Whelan.

At the time I filed, Fr. Whelan was no longer at the school where he had molested me. He was now promoted to Pastor at St. Peter and Paul's church, the largest cathedral in San Francisco, under the ownership by the Diocese of San Francisco, headed and directed by then Archbishop Levada. He was later promoted by the Pope to be the now infamous "Cardinal William Levada," the current Prefect of the Office of the Inquisition, now known as the Congregation of the Doctrine of the Faith, Prefect, and Grand Inquisitor. Same job, different title.

Fr. Whelan was still a Salesian Order priest. The so-called "parish" of St. Peter and Paul's in San Francisco was connected to a Catholic grammar school. I found this fact very disturbing, since I considered this man to be a violent and despicable child molester.

Into the Millennium

In addition to that, several of the Salesian priests on the San Francisco Salesian website were either admitted or convicted molesters, or being sued for child molestation in California by other victims. The Salesian Provincial Mansion, where most of the Salesian priests lived in San Francisco, was almost across the street from Bishop Levada's cathedral near Geary and Franklin Streets.

Finally the pieces of the puzzle predetermined by Karma that I had talked about earlier began to fall into place, but not without anxiety and confusion, and not without the resistance and contempt by the Roman Catholic hierarchy.

Shortly after filing my suit, I began to protest at St. Peter and Paul's church in San Francisco, and at St. Mary's Cathedral, the Cathedral of Cardinal Levada, on several occasions. At one particular event, a Salesian priest had come out of the Cathedral during the protest and told me that I was a liar, that "God" was on their side, and that they would prevail. The Salesians priests, who have been in San Francisco for decades, were a very close-knit group and were very arrogant and aggressive toward protesters of child abuse by their group of child molesters.

I also protested on Peter Yorke Way in San Francisco, which is the headquarters of the Bishop of San Francisco. It was at that time that I met the then Bishop Levada on the sidewalk across the street from his building while I was holding a sign, and he did not know who I was. I blocked his path to try to stop him to tell him that I wanted Fr. Whelan removed from ministry and removed from having access to innocent children at the Catholic grammar school.

A Witch Wins JUSTICE

Bishop Levada did not give me an opportunity to talk; he brushed passed me and called me a "fucking idiot."

So the man who now sits at the Pope's side called me a "fucking idiot" for speaking out loudly against an institution that has caused so much destruction to innocents. I think in retrospect, considering Levada's history, it was a bittersweet compliment; depending on who interprets his angry response. During that time, the Diocese of San Francisco had a so-called "Independent Review Board" of about five members that the Church had established around 2001, that supposedly "reviewed claims of child abuse by clergy" to determine if the claims were "credible or not."

Needless to say, almost all of the claims of child abuse that I knew of against the priests in the Diocese who were working under the jurisdiction of Bishop Levada were determined by this Independent Review Board to be not credible. The first time I made an appointment to go to see Bishop Levada at his office, I was told that he was busy and that Bishop John Wester would see me instead. I went to the Diocese headquarters on Peter Yorke way in San Francisco and went into the office. I saw Bishop Levada in the hallway, and he recognized me with disdain and walked away from me.

Bishop Wester appeared confident that he could convince the group of clergy abuse victims who came with me that my story of abuse was not credible. He spoke with authority.

When I went into the room to see Bishop Wester, he informed me that the Independent Review Board of San Francisco had determined that my claim of sexual abuse by Fr. Whelan was unfounded and not credible. He also said that they had found Fr. Whelan credible instead, and that they had determined that I was fabricating a tale that was not true.

Bishop Wester seemed ecstatic.

"The Independent Review Board found your story not credible," he said.

"What makes a story credible?" I snapped back angrily.

"A credible story has details of what happened," he answered sharply.

His arrogance reminded me personally of the arrogance of the inquisitors, a self-righteous arrogance that was very triggering to me, and at that point I should have left the room.

"You want details?" I heard myself yell out involuntarily at Bishop Wester.

"How would you like to wake up at night because God has a hard on, and he's pissing blood in your face? Is that enough detail?"

Bishop Wester closed his eyes, the vision perhaps too graphic for a supposed holy man. I left the room, shaking violently as I went out the door.

I felt myself slipping...slipping...slipping.

There is a certain feeling many victims get when a person in a position of authority becomes cocky and abusive. It's an unfortunate territory where the boundaries of patience and logic distort, and emotion and pain dictate reactions that fear no consequences.

At a certain place in your life, there are no fears of consequences; you betray your own logic. It's no longer important.

A Witch Wins JUSTICE

For some, this reaction is a side effect of Post Traumatic Stress Disorder. The ability to become invisible and invincible, and not be concerned about the outcome, or even believe in outcomes, overtakes sensibility.

But the room I walked into was the wrong room, and it was too late. It was the chamber. I sunk through the rotten floor and fell eight feet below me into a cavernous black mausoleum.

Jesus was there waiting for me, nailed to the cross. He smiled a wicked smile.

I saw Jesus pull his hands loose from the cross, and the nails ripped his skin open as he yanked his hands off the wood. He fell forward off the cross, and he was laughing at me hysterically.

He had blood all over his hands and his loincloth.

"You're in the wrong room," he roared with continuous laughter.

Then, to be vindictive and spiteful, Jesus held up my bloody underwear that he had saved. He wiped his cuts on the nail holes in his hands with the underwear, and continued laughing.

"Do you have any more underwear," he quipped. "These are too soaking wet."

I fell into the corner of the room, and sat there and covered my head.

"We were just kids," I cried. "You don't even care what you did to us."

"You should have listened to Fr. Purdy, and committed suicide," He laughed.

It serves you right to suffer."

I closed my eyes, and luckily I tasted the saltwater again.

Into the Millennium

"Joey, wake up," Mommy said. She kept shaking me. "You had another nightmare."

I held my mother as tightly as I could, and she comforted me. It was so good to be back home, and realize that it was only a nightmare and it would all go away. She brought me back to my bed and tucked me in gently.

After a while, I looked up at her from my little bed to tell her what had happened.

But Mommy scared me.

Her eyes had that thin film covering them, that undesirable blank stare into the atmosphere. I knew those eyes, and what they meant.

I remembered clearly when Snoopy had those eyes when I was a child, and my cousin Curt had those eyes his last day in the hospital. They didn't move at all; they were cloudy, incapable of any vision, and they didn't blink. They couldn't even shed the saltwater. Mommy stood there lifeless, incapable of saying anything, and I watched her slowly disappear into the atmosphere.

She was gone.

She had passed away five years before I ever talked to Bishop Wester that day. I was alone, and I would never see her again. I had to wake up alone, without Mommy.

I would never be able to tell her how much I had appreciated her saving me all those nights when the saltwater rolled down my face. I would never be able to tell her what happened that day at the school when her own eyes were filled with saltwater, when she thought I was going to be kicked out of school. I would never be able to tell her how I woke up from the nightmares from

A Witch Wins JUSTICE

Salesians, and how I was fighting the evil molesters from the church.

I don't know how I got home that day.

Not long after Bishop Wester told me that the Independent Review Board had found me "not credible," the head of the Independent Review Board Dr. James Jenkins, a psychologist, quit the review board, apparently in disgust. When interviewed by San Francisco Weekly magazine in 2005, Dr. Jenkins said that during his entire tenure, the Independent Review Board had never reviewed my claim of abuse by Fr. Whelan. The Independent Review Board never made any attempt to contact me at all, not to interview me, never to ask me about my molestation claim, because they had never heard my case. Bishop Wester, the tall blond man with the high position under Levada, and now the Bishop of Salt Lake City, had sat next to me calmly and coolly, looked me right in the eye, and lied to *me*—a molestation victim who as a child had been violated by a catholic priest. He wore a large cross around his neck, and I stared at it as he lied to me. The cross sparkled in the light, a shining example of Catholicism, adorned by a warrior for the church, lying to a molestation victim to protect a child rapist. How proud God must have been to witness this!

Seconds later, as I sat there staring at him, I slipped off into a cloudy room, a church somewhere in the past or perhaps in the future, and heard the ghosts of deceased parishioners join me in an acrimonious chant:

"*Let us pray:*

Our Father, who art in heaven, bless Bishop Wester for his loyalty, bless his callous contemptible lies, his protection of child rapists, and his deceit.

And of course, bless the Salesian Society he grants safe harbor to, and the lovely shiny crucifixes that Bishop Wester, Bishop Levada, Fr. Whelan, and all the molester clergy wear. Bless the holy novocaine that numbs child victims, and the wine the clergy abusers drink. Amen."

So in effect, not only did the review board not say that Fr. Whelan had been found credible and that I was not credible, but they didn't even review my case at all.

The "Salesian Society" of clergy, as they were named, who were headquartered in San Francisco on Franklin Street, assumed the role of the defendants in my lawsuit against the Church. Several other victims of Salesian priests also filed lawsuits against the Salesian Society in California in 2003.

The Salesians hired several lawyers and law firms, and seemed to have an infinitely deep pocket for their battle. They ordered depositions of my brothers, sisters, father, distant family, relatives, aunts, uncles, friends, associates, former classmates, and several expert witnesses.

They made it very clear to the public, to my lawyer, and to the media that they were going to fight vehemently, without regard to what they would spend. They hired a professional spokesperson to discredit me to the media, the public, and anybody else who would listen. They hired forensic psychologists to interview and test me, in order to show that I was not credible.

I was deposed by the Salesian team of lawyers in 2004. The leader of this team who was scheduled to depose me was a person whom my tortured soul considered to be a dispassionate, dark-natured woman.

A Witch Wins JUSTICE

She had earned the comical nickname by some of the victims of clergy abuse as "Mrs. Necroni."

My opinion is that she was untouched by the tortured lives of victims of child abuse, because she showed me no emotion whatsoever. She was fitting for the Salesians as an interrogator, and I did not want to know why she assumed the position that she did as the principle interrogator, because I was concerned that it would stir unwanted recollection.

When I arrived to my deposition, I wore my pentacle rings and my pentacle necklace for protection, which apparently went unnoticed by the Salesian gang of interrogators and lawyers. The deposition was triggering, as it brought back ancient memories of the witch interrogations, with merciless interrogators, lacking any sense of emotion or concern.

I was surprised that their two days of endless questioning did not bring the fact that I was a witch to the surface. The Salesian lawyer interrogators never asked me if I was a witch, and I never volunteered the information either. When they interrogated me as to what happened when I was repeatedly molested, they continued to show no emotion whatsoever, which did not surprise me.

They had the same Fr. Purdy monotone suicide-talk voice. Robotic and automatic, devoid of any spirituality. These intelligent lawyers were incapable of seeing me whirl around the room, observing them from the ceiling as I had grown accustomed to doing, and leaving them there talking to a ghost as if they were accomplishing their task, totally unaware of their surroundings. Lawyer inquisitors of the Church become so engulfed in their own fantasy world, they sometimes don't realize the soul they are torturing has already died; and they continue their violations of the abused departed souls of molestation victims, unaware that they can not damage a spirits corpse after it has expired.

No, interrogators, a corpse doesn't bleed.

Perhaps they should teach this morbid phenomenon in law school.

I believe the interrogators were primarily interested in the pursuit of their own financial gains, and not the effects of clergy abuse on Salesian victims.

The Salesian lawyers also deposed my therapist of twenty years, and his files did show that my wife and I had been involved in witchcraft and magick, and that we had also attended "classes" on the same subject. So the truth had leaked out.

After the lawyers discovered the documents that showed my interest in witchcraft and magick, they never questioned me about it. I assumed they would wait for the trial to spring it on me, as if it were a special poison to use for the jury to know that I was not a Christian.

The Magick cat was out of the bag; they knew who and what I was.

Since the lawyers were sharing information with the Diocese, I assumed that Bishop Levada would now know I was a witch, and I also assumed that this would add fuel to our battles. Ironically, Bishop Levada became Cardinal Levada, the modern-day Inquisitor General, the Prefect for the Congregation of the Doctrine of the Faith, the office of the "Hammer of the Witches."

The Salesian lawyers filed motion after motion to try and get my case dismissed on legal technicalities.

A Witch Wins JUSTICE

During the several years that they did this, before the court trial, I would do rituals with other witches to "counter" the conduct of the Church, and my case was never dismissed on a technicality. The Salesians at this point were making public comments as to Fr. Whelan's innocence and their complete assurances that they would prevail in the legal arena. Representatives of the Church said that I was fabricating my tale of being molested by a priest because of my father being abusive, and that I was psychologically disturbed.

Sadly, several of the other victims of Salesian clergy molestation, who had filed suit against the Salesians, represented by the same lawyers representing me, had their cases thrown out. Our lawyers represented most of the clergy abuse cases in Northern California. Yet still, the Salesian lawyers were shamefully successful in having those victims' cases dismissed on various technicalities.

The Salesian Society of priests and brothers was well-known in legal circles as being the most stubborn and unremorseful Catholic order and the most aggressive fighters against child victims they had violated.

I was told on several occasions that the Salesian members of the Church and the "faithful" were praying for Fr. Whelan's victory. My belief, as I stated, is that prayer is arguably a form of magick. And to contradict the magick by Fr. Whelan and the faithful followers and supporters of the man who molested me, I was compelled to perform what is known as "counter magick."

To many Christians and Catholics, the statement that I was performing the Craft of counter magick against the Church and Salesian Order may seem evil or absurd. But I do not think that the officials at the Diocese would

Into the Millennium

consider it as absurd as some parishioners. The Diocese of San Francisco has, to my knowledge, two priests who perform "exorcisms," which is an ancient ritual to exorcise the devil from a person's body or soul.

In other words, the Diocese believes in the practices of the Occult, Magick or Witchcraft, and apparently Satanism. Although I do not believe in Satanism myself, I think the Church considers any form of Witchcraft to be in the same occult "category."

I do know some Catholics and Christians who are scientists that view the practice of magick or witchcraft as not believable. However, this is a contradiction of their own religious ideology if they are true Christians. Their Bible accepts the existence of magick and witchcraft, which is in turn a contradiction to modern science's general belief.

At the many courthouse meetings which were taking place in Oakland and elsewhere, the priests proudly wore their crosses and rosaries, carried their Bibles, and publicly announced their convictions and prayers, and no one questioned whether it was absurd or not. It is generally accepted that clergy do these things, and the public majority does not challenge or confront these practices, probably because Catholicism is the main religion practiced in the United States.

Back at home, I held gatherings and rituals, especially when the moon was full. I invoked "the Mother of Magick," with witches I had known and practiced with, and sometimes I did rituals alone. The rituals were, as stated earlier, to counter the magick by the priests and Bishops and whomever else the Salesians had "praying" for the molester.

A Witch Wins JUSTICE

At this point, we can probably agree that the line between modern beliefs of rationality and ancient beliefs in occultism or Paganism becomes evident. On the one hand, we have Catholic priests clearly practicing the ancient art of prayer to their Saints or God or whatever; and it is for the most part, in today's predominantly Christianity-practicing United States, considered normal.

On the other hand, we have witches practicing the ancient art of magick or witchcraft, and it is for the most part, in today's predominantly Christian United States, considered weird, abnormal or evil.

The double standard is very much alive in the modern United States.

I had made another appointment at the Archdiocese of San Francisco, to meet with the Outreach Coordinator of the Diocese, so that I could gain entry into the building to place an "invocation" in the Bishops office. The invocation was a hand-drawn document, created as a binding spell to counter the evils of the hierarchy who had harbored and protected child abusers.

I believe in symbolism, and so does the Catholic church.

Whether or not this symbolism is outwardly rational is not relevant. The symbolism is a tool for communication with the subconscious mind; therein lies its power.

I left a copy of the hand-drawn symbolic "invocation and binding spell" to Aradia, Diana, and the Mother of Magick in Bishop Levada's office on a table, and he, or they, did not notice when I placed it in the room. Or, if they did notice, I never was made aware of the fact, and they never mentioned it to me. The copy of the document was drawn in black and white. I left it on the table when I entered the office hallway.

In actuality I considered the placement of the invocation in Levada's office both ironic and comical.

After my meeting with the outreach coordinator, I passed by the room and peeked into the office to see if the document was still there. The copy of the invocation was not only still there, but it was colored red. I did a double take and stopped in my tracks. How did the page turn red? I wondered if they made a copy, and used red paper? The outreach coordinator asked me what was wrong and what was I staring at. I turned toward her to say that nothing was wrong and then turned back to look at the document, and it had disappeared. No one was in the room.

I was perplexed and said nothing. I wondered if the document had fallen off the desk at that exact second, or if it had dissolved into the air. My guess is it fell off the table.

I'll never know.

A Witch Wins JUSTICE

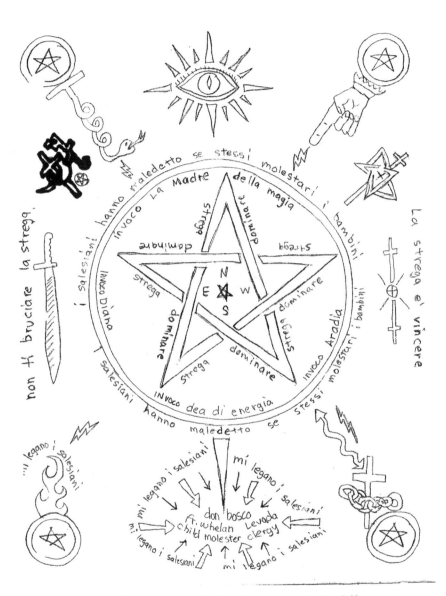

Invocation placed in Cardinal Levada's Office

Into the Millennium

I wrote several letters to Bishop Levada, and the Pope, demanding the removal of the violent predator priest from ministry and demanding they remove him from having access to innocent children, and the Diocese told me that Whelan would stay put in ministry. I considered this deliberately spiteful, not only toward me, but toward all the children exposed to Fr. Whelan.

Cardinal Levada and the Pope seemed to me to be vindictive. They obviously did not have the safety of children at the forefront of their actions.

I sent letters to the "Prefect for the Congregation of the Doctrine of the Faith," which was then Cardinal Ratzinger's title before he became the "Pope Benedict," and he also continuously ignored me. I sent a letter to the Pope with an explanation as to why "the Pope makes me puke." I received no reply.

Ironically, I sent a letter to Cardinal Ratzinger, as the Prefect for the Congregation of the Doctrine of the Faith in January of 2005, shortly before he took the office as the Pope. This so called "Congregation for the Doctrine of the Faith" was, as I stated earlier, the Catholic Church office of the Vatican that was in charge of the Inquisition hundreds of years ago. Cardinal Ratzinger of Germany, who was the head of this office in 2005 while I was suing the Church, knew that he had a role in keeping Fr. Whelan in ministry, as this office was the office that investigated complaints of clergy abuse in the Church. He chose to keep Fr. Whelan at St. Peter and Paul's, despite my continued demands to have Whelan removed. Even more ironically, Cardinal Ratzinger, alias "Pope Benedict," was busted five years later himself for harboring a pedophile

A Witch Wins JUSTICE

priest in Germany, according to reports in March of 2010. My letter to him eerily predicts that occurrence.

Here is a copy of the letter I sent to Cardinal Ratzinger, now known as Pope Benedict, five years before he had been accused of covering up for his own pedophile priest in Germany while he was Bishop there.

Into the Millennium

Jan 5, 2005

Joey Piscitelli
110 Escobar Street
Martinez, CA 94553

Cardinal Joseph Ratzinger
Congregation for the Doctrine of the Faith
Vatican City

Mr. Ratzinger,

As you already know from my prior complaints and active lawsuit, I am a victim of child sexual abuse by one of your disturbed priests, Fr. Steven Whelan, whom you placed in ministry as a Pastor with access to children in San Francisco.

Have you no shame, or sense of decency?

Do you not care about the safety of children? The safety of children in San Francisco and elsewhere should be the most important issue on your agenda. I suspect that you care more about the welfare and security of your abuser priests than that of innocent children, which is a disgrace. To harbor and promote an accused molester to the position of pastor is completely irresponsible. If this is your policy in California, I am sure that you have probably done the same thing in Italy and Germany and elsewhere that you have been located. It's probably just a matter of time that you will get caught yourself, and Karma will catch up to you.

If and when that happens, I hope you will remember me, and all of the others that have demanded that you protect children instead of sexually abusive priests.

A Witch Wins JUSTICE

Your ignoring of my demands to remove the predator that abused me is completely irresponsible, but you already know that. If there is a God, I am sure that he is ashamed of your behavior, and that of all the abusive clergy who are in the Catholic Church.

Joey Piscitelli

As the letter suggested in 2005, Karma would catch up with the Pope, something that I thought was inevitable. His policy of keeping Whelan in ministry, along with that same policy of Cardinal Levada, was consistent with their policies in the past of protecting accused molesters who had access to children. Cardinal Levada was promoted by the Pope to be the new Prefect for the Congregation of the Doctrine of the Faith, announced later in 2005, to take his buddy Ratzinger's place, evidence that the two men were pedophile-protecting peas in a pod, because Levada had a proven reputation of protecting clergy abusers. Levada was truly now the new Grand Inquisitor.

In spite of the behavior of these two irresponsible men, and because of it I continued forward.

I consumed a lot of time and energy focusing on the counter magick Pagan techniques I had acquired or accepted in the last twenty-five years, and I directed my energy toward the binding of the Salesian law teams and Cardinal Levada, and their maneuvers.

None of the relentless legal maneuvers made by the Salesian lawyers to stop my case from proceeding to court worked for them. An argument can be made at this point that it was because my lawyers were doing a good job, and it had nothing to do with Magick whatsoever. That may be one possibility.

Another possibility is that something different was occurring in my case that is not clearly explainable in simple cut-and-dry terms, because the other cases against the Salesian order were all successfully being tossed out of court and dismissed. Perhaps it was a combination of both.

There are no coincidences.

I wrote several articles condemning the behavior of the Salesian nest of pedophiles. The Salesian head lawyer, Steven Mc Feely, appeared to me to be livid when I saw him at various pretrial court motions. Mr. Mc Feely e-mailed me twice, supposedly by mistake, and I saved those e-mails to use in ritual later. The Salesian Order of Priests was infuriated at the articles I wrote where I was naming all the accused molesters and their sordid histories on the internet. I also fed information to magazines and authors about Cardinal Levada's dirty deeds and information about the Salesian nest of pedophiles, which were then copied and printed in large publications. The fact that the information was true prevented the Salesians from having the stories retracted.

During this conflict, the Salesian lawyers continued to try every conceivable angle to have my case dismissed, and they were always unsuccessful at having their motions for dismissal approved by the court.

Because my suit was a suit for psychological or emotional damage as a victim of sex abuse as a minor, the Salesian lawyers were able to force me to go to their own forensic psychologist, who was their paid professional expert "witness." His job was to evaluate me and write a report about me that was obviously supposed to state things about me that would help their case. The forensic psychologist they hired in San Francisco told me that I was going to lose the court case, that my story was not believable, and that I should prepare myself for the worst. I do not think that this man will be rewarded with good Karma.

The Salesian lawyers also made me go to a forensic psychologist in Walnut Creek who also "tested" me, but I do not believe she thought I was a liar. I believe, in fact, that she was an old soul whom I had known far back in the past, and I could sense that she felt something mystical about our meeting.

I told my lawyers at the time that this forensic psychologist woman who "evaluated me" for the Church was not a bad soul, and that she was not like the psychologist in San Francisco. I also stated that I believed she would not show up at the court trial to testify for the Church, because of a feeling I had when I met her. And I turned out to be correct, although the official reason that she did not show up at the trial was never given to me, but it did not matter. I just knew that it would not happen for some reason. It was part of the predestined Karma, I am sure.

The Salesian attorneys scheduled most of the depositions concerning my lawsuit at the law office of my attorney Rick Simons, who was also the lead attorney for most of the Northern California cases, including about eight other Salesian lawsuits.

The depositions for the Salesians were usually led by one of their attorneys named Ms. Nueroni, and another Salesian attorney who I assume despised me as much as I despised him, named Mr. McFeely.

Into the Millennium

One of the most detestable things that the Salesian Attorneys did was to depose my father, to supposedly gain information about me from him that obviously would be used as a tool against me at the trial. The Salesian lawyers were told that he did not know anything about the abuse, was in poor health, and had nothing to offer to the case, for or against me. My father was almost eighty, had already had heart surgery and brain surgery, had heart disease and severe arthritis, and knew nothing about the sexual abuse I had suffered as a child.

The Salesian attorneys were told beforehand he could not hold up well at a deposition, and my lawyers were opposed to them badgering him. Nevertheless they coldheartedly subpoenaed him to a deposition. I brought my poor father to the deposition at the lawyer's office, and he was very emotional and very opposed to going. He was brought into the interrogation room, and I was told to stay outside the building. As the Salesian attorneys badgered him, he began to have a breakdown, which I personally believe was a testament to the attitude of the Salesian attorneys. My father was very devoted to my mother, who at the time of the deposition was deceased. The Salesians knew my mother was deceased, and they knew my father was unstable emotionally and physically. They also knew how devoted my father had been to my mother his whole lifetime, and how hurt he was psychologically and emotionally after her death.

I believe they deposed my father to weaken me, or my case, so that I would be triggered about the incident. I believe there is no limit to far how far some Church lawyers go to weaken victims and their families, and many

A Witch Wins JUSTICE

other victims of sexual abuse by the Church will tell you the same thing.

This conduct by these so-called "religious Catholics" is a further testament to the accusations by many clergy abuse victims of the depravity of the Church hierarchy. After they repeatedly badgered him while he was breaking down, my lawyers objected, and the deposition was called off at that point, and my lawyers refused to allow them to question him anymore. We filed a motion to the court to stop the Salesians from forcing my father to another deposition.

The Church lawyers, however, argued to force him to go through with another deposition.

The hearing for their motion to the court to force my unfortunate, sick father to another deposition was held in Oakland California. I brought another hand-drawn "invocation spell" to the courthouse and placed it on the Salesian attorneys' souls as a binding spell, to protect my father from their further attacks to force him to another deposition. A binding spell is used as a tool by Pagans or Witches to literally "bind" the offensive person(s) from continuing to cause harm to someone. Although it is widely considered superstition or nonsense, it is comparable to writing a prayer to a saint to ask that the saint stop an offensive person from harming you. I placed the "binding spell" in the courtroom, and one of the lawyers scooped it up somehow, an irony perhaps, but it found its way to the intended destination. More symbolism, more craziness—but more success.

My lawyers argued against the wicked motion by the Salesians, and shortly thereafter, the judge ruled that the

Into the Millennium

Salesians could not force my sick father to go to their "interrogation."

I believe the binding spell worked: a testament to the power of the unknown, and the bewilderment of unexplainable magick—energy that logically and rationally should arguably not exist.

The pretrial bickering and sparring by my lawyers and the Salesians went on for three years, and when it was getting close to my trial date, the Salesians informed my lawyer proudly that they had hired a "big shot" lawyer and his firm from Texas, who were going to "mutilate" me in court.

His name was Wayne Mason. They claimed he was the "best of the best." I was under the assumption that Mr. Mason was a hardcore Christian, and I considered him to be a "Bible thumper." He appeared to me to be inundated with self-confidence. I believe his ego was outdone by his arrogance. His ego was also outdone by the sound of thumping on his law books—or perhaps they were Bibles, I couldn't tell.

I saved a picture of Mr. Mason for my future ritual. I also had pictures of Fr. Whelan, Mr. McFeely, and Fr. David Purdy, who was now the head of the Salesian order on the West Coast.

The same Fr. Purdy that I reported in my deposition as having tried to convince me to commit suicide when I was a young teenager, was now the leader of the entire Salesian pack, the so called "Salesian Provincial."

That was another irony.

In addition to these photos, I had pictures of Cardinal Levada, Bishop Niederauer of San Francisco, and Bishop Vigneron of Oakland. I also had a photo of the Pope

A Witch Wins JUSTICE

and a photo of the Salesian founder and supposed-Saint Don Bosco. I kept the photos of all of these clergy and their lawyers along with the Salesian coat of arms shield in my room, so that I could use them in a ritual of magick for the trial. I copied the photos so that I could use them more than once.

At this point, you may wonder about my sanity or whether or not I am delusional; I would expect that. For the record, I do not believe I was abducted by aliens or have psychic abilities that are supernatural. I do not believe in possession by demons or that I have superpowers that make me invincible. But I do believe in the Craft of the Wise.

And Karma.

And I believe in the energy of the universe that can be manipulated by magick.

Consider this:

Fr. Whelan molested me several times when I was an innocent minor. He held a high position in the Catholic Church in San Francisco, under Cardinal Levada. Cardinal Levada refused to take him out of ministry, even though Fr. Whelan was being sued for child molestation, because the Cardinal *expected* the Church to win the trial. The Cardinal had been promoted right before my trial to be the top man at the Vatican, sitting at the Pope's side. It goes without saying that the Pope must have known about my case, which directly involved the famous Cardinal and his prized priest, Fr. Whelan.

I sent many letters to Cardinal Levada and the Pope, complaining about the abuser they promoted to Pastor with access to children, and they fell on deaf ears. The Diocese also supposedly forwarded some of my letters of complaint, and they were also ignored. I also complained to the Congregation of the Doctrine of the Faith, which was a joke. They (especially Cardinal Levada), totally ignored me.

It is a pretty fair assumption that Cardinal Levada, the Pope, the new Bishop of San Francisco Bishop Niedereuer, the Bishop of Oakland, Bishop Vigneron, and all the Salesian clergy and many of their parishioners and supporters were probably all <u>praying</u> for Fr. Whelan to win the trial. The Pope *expected* Fr. Whelan to win, because the Pope and Cardinal Levada believed they had a direct line to God.

The hierarchy's magick (prayer), as far as I know, is considered by tens of millions to be the ultimate magick of the Catholic Church.

But Magick has no boundary.

There are no rules, and as far as I am concerned, there was an evil and an injustice that had been done, that I believe magick can cure. Magick can change the results, despite the conjuring of any God by any Pope or hierarchy of any church, any clergy, or any one of the millions of their "faithful."

The blending of magick and Karma is superlative.

I myself met many faithful Catholics at church protests I organized before my trial who told me that they were "praying" for Fr. Whelan to win his case in court.

I did not understand why some would come out of the churches and yell and curse at me, and also yell at the other protesters who had shown up to protest against the clergy abusers. They would tell me that God was on Fr. Whelan's side, as they did years earlier when I first filed my lawsuit. Many said that they were all praying

A Witch Wins JUSTICE

in Catholic churches everywhere for him. That confused me. What should have been foremost on anyone's mind is whether or not other children who were exposed to Fr. Whelan were safe.

One priest told me at a protest at St. Peter and Paul's Cathedral that, and I quote:

"You are going to realize that the power of Catholic prayer is invincible, and you are going to learn the hard way that you do not mess with our Lord Jesus Christ and his sacred Salesian priests."

I believe the name of Jesus Christ should not be spoken in the same sentence as Salesian priests.

Prayer, as I keep stressing, is a form of magick.

Because the Catholic Church is so large, it is common for millions of Catholics to "pray" on a regular basis, not realizing that praying is in fact the practice of magick, which is not allowed by the teachings of the church. Not only that, many of the Catholic faithful continue to pray to dead saints and a dead God, which is a form of conjuring, which their church strictly forbids.

But if a witch practices magick, the church considers it an abomination.

In addition to that, if a witch practices magick, many people consider the witch to be some kind of deranged psycho. But many of the people who consider witches to be senseless kooks are the same people who practice magick themselves by "praying" to those said dead saints for favors, but they continue for some reason to consider their prayers rational.

Many witches adhere to "the Threefold Law," which in effect means that if you do magick to harm someone, it will come back to you threefold. There are two arguments that come to my mind that I would like to present here.

One argument is that if I performed "Black Magick" to harm Fr. Whelan and the Church, it would come back to me threefold.

The second argument here is that if the Church and all of its clergy performed Black Magick to harm me, it would come back to them threefold.

I do not believe both the church and I could suffer the consequences of "the threefold law"; and more importantly, as I already proclaimed, I believe I was tortured in a past life by the church, and I was molested in this life by the present Church. The Church in the present, and in the past, has already done harm to me.

Which brings me to this conclusion: the church was in fact performing black magick in the form of "sacred prayer to a god," intentionally meant to harm me again, and they were destined to face the consequences for it. The Pope, Cardinal Levada, Fr. Whelan, and other members of the Catholic prayer syndicate were, in my opinion, casting evil intentions.

The next thing I offer is this: I was entitled to perform dark counter magick against the oppressors of the church, and I felt justified in the act, which was an act of defense.

Shortly before my trial began in 2006, the Bishop of Oakland, Allen Vigneron, held special "Apology Services" at different churches and schools in the Bay area, for political purposes, to show that he supposedly cared for the victims of abuse in the Oakland Diocese. The media ate this up, and Bishop Vigneron went to each Parish church and said a mass and apology to all

A Witch Wins JUSTICE

the victims from that church that had been molested by priests at those locations. He mentioned the names of some of the priests who had been sued, and mentioned the names of some of the abuse victims who wanted to be apologized to publicly at these services.

I contacted Allen Vigneron and told him that I was abused by Fr. Whelan at Salesian school. Vigneron told me that at his very last apology service at the church in San Ramon in 2006, before my trial, he would mention all of the victims of Salesian priests, and he would apologize to me in front of hundreds of people for what Fr. Whelan had done to me, and he would make sure that I was personally mentioned. He also said he would mention the names of all the priests at Salesian who were accused of molestation or were being sued by claimants.

I went to the service with about fifteen other victims, and I waited during the service for Vigneron to mention Fr. Whelan and the other clergy abusers from Salesian school. I waited for him to mention my name and to apologize to me for Whelan's crimes against me.

Bishop Vigneron did not mention Fr. Whelan or the other abusers at Salesian, nor did he mention my name or apologize to me, as he had promised.

I walked up the aisle of the church in front of the entire congregation, and I interrupted the service. I reminded the Bishop that he did not mention Whelan or apologize to me, and that he did not mention all of the other Salesian victims, or the abusers from Salesian that those victims had accused of abuse. Vigneron was silent. I called him a coward in front of hundreds of people at the service.

Into the Millennium

While I was walking down the aisle to leave the church after my interruption of the service, many people stood up to give me a standing ovation. Most of the victims in the pews in the crowd at the church left the service when I did, and thanked me for being so brave. Bishop Vigneron's secretary later said that he did not mention my name because either he did not know who I was or he "forgot." I wrote to Bishop Vigneron in a letter that in the future, I would always make sure that he would remember who I was.

The Court Trial

In July of 2006, I appeared at a court meeting with my lawyer Rick Simons in Contra Costa County Court to meet the judge before my trial. The Salesian Catholic lawyers were there in mass numbers also. The judge gave pretrial instructions, and the Salesian lawyer team's head honcho and braggart, Mr. Mason, told the judge:

"Mr. Piscitelli does not have a shred of evidence whatsoever."

The Judge replied that "Mr. Piscitelli **is** the evidence in his case."

Mr. Mason smiled and looked at me. I felt as though I was being mocked. His expression reminded me of an expression of a church official, one whom I had seen in my previous lifetime.

It was a despicable, condescending moment.

The official I saw was ready to put a witch on trial, and he was completely sure of himself and his righteous mission for the church.

My lawyer had met the Salesian lawyers outside of the courtroom to talk about a "settlement." The Salesian lawyers scoffed at him and told him they were going to beat him in court and that they were not willing to settle for even a dime.

They were there for the slaughter.

They stated that they were absolutely sure of victory, with no compromise.

A Witch Wins JUSTICE

My lawyers seemed worried. I had no witnesses, and of course no documents, videos, or any technical or tangible evidence of any kind to speak of.

I only had my word.

The Salesian files on their nest of accused abusers was remarkably "empty." The judge said that I was not allowed to mention any of the names of the other Salesian molesters from my school at the trial, because it would poison the jury. This was very much in favor of the Salesians' case, as it would make it appear to the jury that Fr. Whelan was the only accused molester at my school. Their lawyers seemed ecstatic over this ruling. It gave them a tremendous advantage to hide this information from the jury.

The Salesians had spent an insane amount of money to build their case, and all I had was my memory, and my story, which all of the Salesian clergy disputed. I was very much outnumbered; but truth, I felt, contains its own power.

I also felt they had wanted to make an example out of me. At the time of my trial, I had been already responsible for several protests all over the State of California to oust accused pedophiles from many different churches.

I had stirred so much controversy with the public and the media that several priests were removed from their positions, and in some cases they were removed from ministry altogether. I had been on radio and TV several dozen times, and my name had appeared in newspapers and magazine articles at least fifty times in the four years before the trial.

This did not sit well with the hierarchy of the church. I had arranged for my sister to serve a subpoena on

The Court Trial

Cardinal Levada himself at his final mass celebration at the cathedral in San Francisco, and my brother had served a subpoena on him with a lawsuit for another victim. It was a war.

And the Salesians made a very special effort to spend as much time, money, and energy as possible to make this court trial the ultimate war against an opposing advocate leader such as I was. And they were fighting for much more than Fr. Whelan's reputation. They were also fighting for the church, Cardinal Levada, the entire Salesian Society, and the Salesian community universally. They had a barrage of lawyers, experts, computer crews, video people, assistants—you name it.

It became a Catholic condemnation circus.

The bragging I heard about the anticipated Salesian victory reached a record high, and the premature victory celebrations were bursting at the seams. But most of all, as another very outspoken, cocky priest had said at one of our protests,

"Saint Don Bosco, Jesus Christ, and Almighty God himself are on our side. We know our prayers will not be ignored."

I saw priests and supporters with rosary beads and Bibles at the courthouse, practicing their magick intently and as seriously as possible, equally sure of that victory. I am convinced that they too still believed firmly that their "God" and their "Saints" would never let them down.

The trial was scheduled to last over a week, as the church has scheduled many people to testify; several priests, forensic psychologists, Fr. Whelan, Fr. Purdy, Brother Sal, and many of their so called experts. My lawyers suggested at that time that I should not attend the

A Witch Wins JUSTICE

trial when all the other witnesses and experts were on the stand, because they had thought that I would be traumatized by the Salesian "circus."

Because I had suffered many years with PTSD, their suggestion was a good idea. The first two days of court, I did not attend. The Salesians examined some of the witnesses, experts, and priests on the stand to show what a liar I was. Their lead attorney, Mr. Mason, put my wife on the stand to admit that we were into magick and witchcraft. This, I have no doubt, was purely for the purpose of poisoning the conservative jury with the idea of how evil and non-Christian I was.

He seemed very proud as he brought out the fact to the jury. Neither the judge nor my lawyer intervened or objected to Mr. Mason doing this. I am sure that Mr. Mason was violating my constitutional rights, as his intent was to convince the jury that a person who is non-Christian and a witch was a person that was not a credible witness.

Because there were so many clergy, Bishops, Salesians, and Catholic faithful still intently praying their magick for Whelan, I was compelled to do my own magick at home. I had'nt been on the witness stand yet.

In spite of those who believe the Craft of Magick is an illusionary waste of time and effort, I maintain my certitude that the Pagan practice is valid. Others may feel that desperate people do desperate things and that the reliance upon the mystical powers of unseen forces is a substantiation of that hopelessness.

If in fact that theory is justified, then I would be thrust into the category of the majority of the population of the United States, 80 percent of whom have at one time

The Court Trial

or another ultimately resorted to magick in the form of prayer to relieve their desperation.

However, I regard the practice of magick and Pagan arts as directly irrespective of the "Black Art" of the prayers by Catholic hierarchy to protect child abusers, and I believe the magick I practice to be necessary for the benefit of seeking justice for those who have been violated. And to be more contradictory, I believe the art of Pagan Magick is not prayer as it is in a Christian sense. I believe it is manipulation of will and energy.

During the trial I used my downstairs room at my house as my magick room. In the center of the room was a small round table. I placed a pentacle in the center of the table. I placed the pictures of Whelan, his Provincial Fr. Purdy, his lawyers Mason and McFeely, and Don Bosco, Cardinal Levada, and the Pope around the pentacle in a circle. I cast the Witches' circle in the room, and I invoked the Mother of Magick to interfere with the trial.

Arguably delusional? Perhaps, but necessary.

Take into account that the modern practice of medicine, which is based on scientific methods and constant testing procedure, is ever changing and has dramatically evolved and improved itself consistently throughout the centuries. Yet many doctors will agree that the key to many symptoms, ailments, and diseases is based in the mind, and that the mind has the ability to trick or deceive the body by the utilization of an invisible force within itself.

Skeptics have no choice but to concede that this phenomenon, which years ago would have been regarded as witchcraft or magick, is now admitted to

A Witch Wins JUSTICE

be "science." I maintain that the process is still magick and always has been.

The problem with the supposed present-day logical conclusions is that many of the professional "experts" who share the opinion that witchcraft and magick are irrational, believe that the organized Catholic Church, which has been inundated with rapes, tortures, murders, and manipulation and molestation of millions of innocents for over a thousand years, is still operating with a rational belief system.

Given those facts, I practice the Craft of Magick with no reservations.

It is my opinion that the Catholic group of people I mentioned above who were praying and fighting against me were, in fact, still performing their sordid acts of "Black Magick"; that is, magick for the continued causes of evil and harm to occur to a victim or victims of clergy abuse. Their black magick is still contained in their prayers, although they will dispute this.

I do know that there are also many witches and magickians who believe that there is no such thing as "Black Magick." That is to say, those witches believe that magick is magick; it is neither "black" nor "white."

I understand this theory.

But I think it's only semantics. For the sake of clarity and convenience, if someone is performing magick for an unjust cause or an unjustified result, or to harm someone, I will call that practice the practice of Black Magick.

I will call the practice of magick for a noble or good cause, or that causes harm to no one, "White Magick." And I will call the practice of reversing Black Magick against an evil intentioned entity, "Dark counter

Magick." But I still agree that magick is magick, whatever the shade.

The trial went on day after day as the priests continued to pray and hold their rosaries and bibles and I continued to practice dark counter magick. Their prayers were still unjustified. I believe when you are a victim, or a target of those who perform their evil craft "in the name of God," you are left with little or no alternatives.

Whether or not anything is acceptable or anyone is "normal," what matters in court when the verdict is read is who wins. I was determined, for the sake of my past and my present incarnation, to find the justice I sought, no matter what anyone thought of the magick I was compelled to practice. As they say, the proof is in the pudding.

My lawyers had repeatedly told me:

"You are the whole case. We have no documents, no witnesses who were there on your side, and no evidence. You are the whole of the case."

I am sure my lawyers did not believe in witchcraft or magick (irrespective of their knowledge of the revelations by modern medicine to coincide with ancient magickal beliefs); and I did not bother to ask them. And ironically, lawyers practice the art of magick whether they believe it is magick or not. They cause change to occur with will all the time. It is what lawyers do, and they do not realize they practice the art almost on a daily basis. It's probably more accurate to state that they do not practice any forms of ancient Magickal ritual or Witchcraft *knowingly*.

When my lawyers came to my house after the third day of court to tell me that it was my turn to testify the

A Witch Wins JUSTICE

next day, they seemed overwhelmed. They told me that Mr. Mason and the Salesian lawyers had thrashed my therapist and my family and that my case looked very dim. My lawyers were very pessimistic.

But this battle was predestined, and I was convinced of that. I know it is a waste of breath to tell a lawyer that you believe you will win a case because of magick, so needless to say, I did not bother. I know you cannot tell your lawyer that you are a reincarnated witch, and that the law of cause and effect, and Karma have predestined your outcome, so needless to say I did not do that either.

Most modern witches adhere to the tenet, "And harm ye none, do as thou wilt."

I agree with this. But the tenet does not go on to say that when a gun barrel is pointed in your face, you should eat the bullets.

I decided to do a dark ritual at that point in the trial that I am sure would have caused some witches to leave the room, but on the same token, I do not believe what the Pope, the Cardinal, and the clergy were continuing to do was acceptable. And the cockiness and arrogance of their lawyers was now over the top. Maybe we're all delusional, and maybe we're all abnormal. And maybe that levels the playing field. Or perhaps, it levels the battlefield.

In actuality, none of us are normal, are we?

There is a certain mystique that is captivating about delusional art, an art that dissipates into an imaginative powder, a mist that covers the facade of reality that we consider "normal." Its ambivalence is its appeal.

The Court Trial

We're all in fact "energy"; we come from energy, and unto energy we return. There is no normal energy or abnormal energy.

Energy is energy, period.

In any case, I did more magick ritual, and the Catholic hierarchy did more magick ritual. It had gotten past the point of merely waiting for justice to prevail by itself; it was now a full blown "witch trial," as Mr. Mason had pointed out to the jury of our involvement with the Craft. And I had already learned my lesson about Church "fairness" in my past life. The lesson I had been taught in my past about Church fairness with Witches was: *there is none*.

It came to my mind at this point that many of the new Pagan books that you see on the shelves of bookstores today state that they are books about "the dark side of the craft," "Dark Magick," and so on. I own many of these books, and I have read many of them. They have nothing in them that suggests to me they are written about "Black Magick." They do not contain anything in them that I even consider dark, for that matter.

Not that I believe that they should contain Black Magick; my point is the that true Black Magick was in the courtroom. And in the hierarchy of the Catholic Church. And I was not going to be tortured and killed again by the arrogance or hatred of people who claimed to be working in the name of "the one true God Almighty."

Once again I set up my table and put the pictures of the Catholic lawyers and clergy around the pentacle on the table. I cast the circle, and I tranced to the disappearance of time, sound, and the past. This time I invoked Aradia, Diana, the Mother of Magick, and,

A Witch Wins JUSTICE

Jesus Christ the Jewish Magickian himself, to defy the vindictive clergy.

I knelt before the table, and I quoted this verse from the ***Il vangelo della strega*** **(Aradia, Gospel of the Witches):**

Quando un prete ti fara del male,
Del male colle sue bene di'Zione,
Tu le farei sempre un doppio male,
Col mio nome, col nome di Diana,
Regina della streghe...

It means:

And when a priest shall do you injury,
By his benedictions, you shall do to him,
Double the harm, and do it in the name,
Of me, Diana, Queen of Witches all.

I interpreted it to mean that someone who has been harmed by a priest would reverse the harm and send it back to the priest, to deal with the deserved fate and consequences.

After saying this verse, I placed the pictures of the Pope, the Cardinal, St. Bosco, the priests and their lawyers, in my metal cauldron in the center of the table, and I lit them on fire. I also burned copal incense. I closed my eyes to trance. Whether or not this type of conduct is considered acceptable, rational, or delusional is of no consequence or matter to me.

Sometimes the word "delusion" magickally becomes the word "delicious."

The Court Trial

It is what it is.

I do not know how long my eyes were closed—it could have been minutes or hours, I will never know. Such is the sensation of the absence of time. I may have been in a deep trance, or maybe I fell asleep. I thought I was dreaming, but I realized I was floating on the kitchen ceiling, and I fell backward into the dark night full of stars. I kept falling backward, and I had the strongest urge to get back home again, when I saw glimpses of the witch trial. The trial was the new trial, not the old one. I saw Mr. Mason and Fr. Purdy. I was frightened, and I shook myself vigorously to wake up.

When I woke up, I ran back into Mommy's room, and it was smoky. I tried to tell Mommy about Fr. Whelan, and she did not understand. My father woke up and took me back to bed.

"Don't worry Joey," he said. "There is no man that's going to hurt you when you go to school."

I tried to tell my Daddy that I dreamed that I was in the future, but I did not know what the future was. I realized that some of my nightmares were about the priests in the future, but I had no way to present the story to Mommy or Daddy. Daddy went back into his bedroom. I could hear him talk to Mommy.

"I don't know what that kid is talking about," he said. "He's half asleep babbling about a priest who hurt him. He's says it's smoky in the room. I didn't see any smoke."

"He'll be Ok," Mommy returned. "He just needs to go back to sleep."

I went back to sleep, and I woke up again, and it was still smoky. It smelled like copal incense. I was floating over the room for a while, and I slowly opened my eyes wider. The strange colorful smoke completely filled the room. It lingered about the room for several minutes and hovered over the center of the room in odd shapes. Instead of dissipating, the smoke seemed to drop back down into the cauldron.

The room was clear all of a sudden. The pentacle was still on the round table, and my wife must have still been at the courthouse. It was odd. I took the ashes, which were all that was left of the pictures of the Salesians and their lawyers, out of the cauldron. The ashes were now charged by Diana, Aradia, and the Mother of Magick. I placed them into a little cobalt bottle.

At this point you may be wondering if I drink excessively, take drugs, or smoke anything. I do not. I practice magick, and I trance into the other world, devoid of time, and devoid of rules and boundaries. This is where the fine lines between reality, PTSD, and memory dissolve, and the colors of light are so beautiful, and are so misunderstood, yet they are so delightful.

To bathe in the art of supposedly delusional magick is comparable to dancing in the sky of energy and bliss, a surrealistic world in all its splendor. It is far beyond the prison of material entrapment, the temporary earthly world that is the real illusion.

I took the bottle of "charged" ashes with me to court the following day.

Magick is as Magick does.

The next day I was put on the stand, and my impression of Mr. Mason was that he was smirking at me, full of himself, as though he had already won the case. He asked me how I was abused, and I felt my PTSD kicking in. It was not controllable. Mr. Mason had been

The Court Trial

transformed in my own mind as the Inquisitor General, and he seemed to me to be enjoying his performance in the courtroom.

He looked up and pointed in a theatrical fashion and said,

"Do you believe in OUR LORD JESUS CHRIST?"

He knew I did not, because of my answer to that very question at my deposition. I imagine he was still trying to poison the jury into hating me. My lawyer should have objected, because a person's religious preference should not be brought against them in court. As I stated earlier, I am sure it was unconstitutional to try to poison a conservative Christian jury by pointing out that a person on the stand was a Pagan. His presence was so disturbing, as it was reminiscent of the righteous, loud witch prosecutor I had memories of in the past, screaming the name of "the Lord Jesus Christ" while the veins bulged from his neck.

He was a very haunting figure to me.

I felt as though I had been cast in a horror movie, and the movie was about my past life at a witch interrogation, and I tried desperately to avoid the memories.

I answered him anyway.

I said "No." "Not in a Catholic sense."

He smirked.

Mr. Mason then went on asking questions about the molestation, while smirking and mocking me, and I slipped into my post-traumatic stress world. It was a familiar place. Possibly he may have wanted me to. I do not know what happened at that point.

I was back several hundred years ago at the witch trial, and I was back into a nightmare of being molested

A Witch Wins JUSTICE

by God, or the priest, I do not know. When I looked at him all I saw in my own mind was an evil inquisitor at the witch trial. He laughed while I went crazy. The laughing echoed louder, and louder, and louder, until I could not stand it any longer.

I may have blacked out.

I felt as I did just before I was tortured and burned in my past life. My skin was crawling; I seemed to be melting. It had all come back at once. I was truly back on the trial stand. I had taken leave of the present and of where I was in time. In fact there was absolutely no sense of time whatsoever, which could have been the result of the PTSD, or the magickal working itself, I do not know.

I believe that Magickal Karma had taken control of the room.

I had waited hundreds of years for this.

I began to float around the room, and I could smell and taste the moldy damp stone walls of the torture chamber again. I heard the cries of women and children, and I heard the sound of chains wrapped around the witches' arms and legs rattling through the room. It was cold and dark, and Mr. Mason's voice echoed again through the chamber hideously while his laughter made me nauseous, and I could see blood splatter on his clothes as I hovered over him. I heard children's bones cracking, but the lawyers didn't even flinch. The sound of each crack caused a spray of blood to spatter across the room.

The lawyers didn't notice the blood at all. It sprayed across the judge's desk, and the judge ignored it. The chains were dripping, and it affected the sound of the metal hitting the stone and dirt floors.

The Court Trial

The proceedings went forward in broken frames; voices came from everywhere, out of the walls, the floors, the benches; and time jumped forward and backward randomly. The judge told me to step down, and his head was covered in a dark hood, and words seemed to come out of his mouth in a slow drawl. I couldn't look at him; the scene was going to cause me to vomit. I held it in.

As I stepped off of the witness stand, in front of the jury, my legs were buckling from under me. I yelled at Mr. Mason and Mr. McFeely in the courtroom, in front of the jury loudly:

"YOU'RE SUPPOSED TO BE PEOPLE OF GOD!"

It was just as I had yelled out at my witch trial hundreds of years ago when I was being tortured to death, the exact same words that I had yelled at the inquisitor and torturer at the trial chamber. The blood was still being relentlessly spattered everywhere, and I could smell death in the room.

"YOU'RE SUPPOSED TO BE PEOPLE OF GOD!"

I knew I was repeating the words again from my memory at the witch trial.

I thought maybe I said:

"Si suppone di essere popolo di Dio!"

I was confused. I think I was speaking in Italian.

I clearly recalled those exact words from the chamber, and I recalled them from the recurring nightmares as a child. I knew I had memories of dreams as a child that were actually also memories of this same trial, and I was unable to tell the trials apart from each other now, and the time frames kept reversing. I was amazed that I could recall that the confusing dreams as a three-year-old had included this very trial day and the people in this courtroom. No wonder I couldn't explain it to Mommy.

My lawyers stared at me in panic. I could see that they thought I might be hallucinating. I tried desperately to control the disorder, and I attempted to walk out of the courtroom.

The words seemed to come out of my mouth involuntarily, and I couldn't escape or shake off the feeling of the agonizing witch torture room, and the past recollection of the suffering and the scene of the nightmare hundreds of years ago, nor of the nightmares from when I was a child.

"*You're supposed to be people of God,*" I yelled in the courtroom again. "*I was just a kid.*"

The Salesian lawyers stared at me in disbelief. So did my own lawyers.

I felt as though I was trying to wake myself up and tell myself the trial wasn't real, and I would run back into my Mommy's bedroom. I tried to pull my bedsheet blanket over my head, and hide and wait until the nightmare was over, but it was useless.

I kept waking up to see the courtroom.

Then I noticed someone was holding me up. The jury was shocked at my behavior.

All of a sudden I realized that I was being removed from the courtroom, and the judge was angry. I was taken from the courtroom into a waiting room to calm down. The court was ordered into a recess. As I sat at a large table surrounded by many chairs, my lawyers came into the room and yelled at me. They said that the case was going terribly before I had gone ballistic, and

The Court Trial

now they were sure I had blown it. They kept insisting I had lost the case, but I did not believe that.

I looked at them in a blank stare and said, "No, I won't lose."

They were confused as to why I thought I could possibly have any chance of winning after what I had done. The room was spinning, and I heard their voices in my ears as though they were whispers that seemed to be drifting away from me as they spoke. There was a strange hiss in my head, and I could not tell if it was a headache or not; it felt similar to jet lag. The hissing was blanking out their voices more and more as they yelled at me. My ears were hurting.

I closed my eyes, and I opened them again at Salesian School in 1972.

I was on the floor of the English classroom, and Brother Dan had just punched me in my ear. I had just awakened from being knocked unconscious, and my ear was bleeding, and I had a ringing hissing sound that carried through both ears. Some classmates carried me into this room, and I had to shut my eyes and hold my throbbing deaf ear. I opened my eyes again, and I was staring at my lawyers sitting at the table, still yelling at me. I put my finger into my left ear and then removed it. There was still blood on it. I stared at my lawyers, who didn't realize that I could not hear out of my left ear, or why it was bleeding.

There was no way I could describe to them what had happened, and I surely was not going to tell them that I was traveling though timelessness because of magick; they would have hauled me off to the loony bin. But I was still in a traumatic daze.

A Witch Wins JUSTICE

I do not know why my educated lawyers were unable to identify the real-life symptoms of PTSD, occurring there in the courtroom in front of their face. It seemed that they only felt frustration, perhaps out of stress, or fear of losing the case, I do not know. It also occurred to me that there are very striking similarities between occult magickal travel, and trauma, and the effects of energy gone wild.

After several minutes, I was brought back into the courtroom, and I was put on the stand again. I was still not stable, and I didn't care anymore, so I did not tell them I was in the condition that I was in.

It was useless to try to explain to the church lawyers Mr. McFeely and Mr. Mason that you can't kill a corpse and that a dead soul cannot bleed. They wouldn't understand.

It didn't matter anyway; magick would just work its own way.

Mr. Mason still seemed to me to be full of himself. He displayed a picture of Fr. Steve Whelan's office on the courtroom wall on a giant screen for the jury to see. The photo showed a clear glass door and several large clear glass windows in the walls of Fr. Whelan's office. He was attempting to show the jury that my story of being molested in the office on a few occasions was impossible because of the abundant visibility of the interior of the office.

"Is this Fr. Whelan's office that you said you were molested in, in broad daylight at the school in the middle of the day?" he smirked.

He looked in the jury's eyes for effect and seemed confident.

The Court Trial

I looked at the photo on the screen, and I was confused. It was Whelan's office. But the picture seemed wrong. I didn't answer Mason.

"Is this his office?" he commanded.

"There's something wrong," I answered bluntly.

"Answer the question," the judge demanded.

I lost my sense of hearing again for a moment. I was looking toward my lawyer, sitting at a desk in the middle of the courtroom. He appeared to be frustrated at my refusal to answer the question. But as I stared toward him at his desk, something odd caught my eye. Below him, I was distracted by the bundle of papers and books on the floor at his desk side. They were moving by themselves.

I was mesmerized and dumbfounded.

It appeared as though my High School yearbook wiggled out of the bundle by itself and fell to the floor. The hair stood up on my neck, and I looked at my lawyer and the others around the courtroom, and nobody had seemed to notice the bizarre occurrence. Perhaps my lawyer had unintentionally kicked the yearbook out from the bundle?

The yearbook pages flipped open and stopped at a certain page. I was straining to see the page, which was impossible, while the judge kept repeating his command to me to answer the question. I couldn't hear him clearly, and he must have been very angry at that point. I didn't care what the judge was saying anyway.

"There's something wrong," was all I said.

I could not explain the yearbook scene; it was too mystifying. There was no way I would mention it to anyone at this point, considering all that had happened already.

A Witch Wins JUSTICE

"Tell your client to answer the question," the judge told my lawyer.

My lawyer called for a recess.

"What are you doing?" he said.

"There's something wrong with the picture," I said. "We need to look in the yearbook."

"What's in the yearbook?" he questioned.

I couldn't explain.

We rifled through the yearbook, and in the middle of the yearbook, at about the page that had opened in the courtroom, was a photo of Fr. Whelan's office. The door and the glass windows were opaque. It was impossible to see through them.

"We will enter these photos as evidence," my lawyer said. "The windows and glass must have been changed since you left the school, and are now clear windows."

The Salesian lawyers were trying to deceive the jury.

When we returned to the courtroom, the Salesian supporters seemed to be already in celebration. The judge said to me that I had really damaged my case severely, but I did not believe him. I was sure that I would win, but I could not say why. It was a sensation, not describable or verifiable, like the different colors of the air that I could now see in the room.

We introduced the pictures of the office glass as evidence, but it did not faze the Salesians—they seemed to be overwhelmed with the sense of victory regardless of any testimony. It was reminiscent of the witch trials: no matter what the evidence, or how wrong the Church was, the inquisitors knew they would win, irrespective of any material facts that were presented. They had never changed.

The Court Trial

I was questioned a few times more by Mr. Mason, who at this time seemed as though he could hardly contain himself. His admiring fans in the courtroom were congratulating each other as though their victory had already been announced. The priests were thanking their Lord Jesus Christ and making the sign of the cross in recognition of their surety of their majestic verdict. They were kissing their Bibles and looking up toward the sky and thanking Jesus repeatedly, and they appeared to be teary eyed with satisfaction. But I could still see and feel the energy in the room. They were blind to it.

Then time disappeared again.

I looked at the jury, and they would not look back at me. None of them would look me in the eyes; they couldn't. They seemed to be in a trance themselves. An eerie sense of disorientation filled the room as before, and I felt as though I was being pulled back into the witch torture trial yet again. I recalled that in the past, after the agony and the pain had gone so far, I had entered a surreal place where there was no sound, no feeling, and no sense of human sensation.

Like an overdose of that novocaine again.

I was very familiar with this reaction. I remembered that the colors in the air in the room of the witch trial chamber seemed to turn to just red and the room became smoky. It was what I saw hundreds of years ago, and it was here again. I had thought that the "traveling" into timelessness and the past was over, but it wasn't. How long would this keep happening? There are no rules for magick and PTSD; perhaps their marriage is a disguised blessing.

A Witch Wins JUSTICE

I started to travel yet again, but it was different this time. I felt "high" and absolutely full of energy, and I felt I had entered a different plane than before. I had the same sensation of floating about the room, as though I was being traumatized again. There was still no pain and still no feeling at all, just existence. It seemed much more peaceful, in spite of the circumstances.

The people in the room were frozen in space, and they had no expression, as though they were suspended because the next frame of linear time was on hold. I could float above them and around them, and I could see myself sitting on the stand, as frozen as they were. I watched us all in amazement. None of us had expression, and I watched myself as I did when I was born, and as I did when Whelan molested me at the multipurpose room, and as I did at the witch trial hundreds of years ago.

The Mother of Magick was present.

Perhaps this is how the spell of Karma works. Einstein was correct: you can be in more than one place at one time. Time stops when you travel at the speed of light, or when you become traumatized. That absence of time allows the peculiarities that defy regulations of science. It allows magick to occur.

Somehow the proceeding did continue, and I stepped down from the witness stand again, but still there was no sound at all, and still no pain, and the room was hazy.

Mr. Mason was transparent. I could see through his skin, and I could see his skeleton, and his blood pumping through his translucent skin. His blood seemed to be black, like the hood covering his head. His eyes were missing, a testament to his blindness of the magick. How fitting.

I noticed that the bottle of ashes in my pocket felt hot. I withdrew the bottle and instinctively spread the ashes into the courtroom which I had collected from my ritual at home, and I realized that I could be reprimanded for such conduct.

I suddenly regretted spreading the ashes in front of all the people in the courtroom, I was afraid I could go to jail as a consequence. The ashes slowly spread in the air, and I was concerned that they were taking too long to dissipate. But I looked around, and no one saw me. It was amazing that no one could see the ashes; perhaps they were invisible to them, and perhaps the jury was still in some kind of spell, or in an altered state themselves. Or, perhaps they all just didn't notice anything unusual.

I watched the magick-charged ashes spread through the room, like a pale purple mist, unbelievably unnoticed. The ashes circled around Mr. Mason, Mr. McFeely, and the priest, and they were completely blind. I saw the purple mist hover around the jury, and I was worried it would make them angry and insulted. They seemed to inhale the mist, which truly frightened me. I looked at the judge for a reaction, and he had none. The Salesian lawyers had no reaction either. The bailiff was frozen with no reaction at all. Everyone in the room still had the same blank stare, as if they were still not awake. No one at all seemed to be mentally present to see all the ashes scatter across the courtroom. It may have lasted a second, or perhaps a minute, but the clock had certainly stopped, and I kept waiting for the ashes to dissipate.

A Witch Wins JUSTICE

As the ashes finally settled to the floor, sound returned to the room.

I waited for the consequences and anticipated that the judge would have me ejected from the court. But nothing happened.

People had expressions on their faces again. Linear time had returned.

I know very well the parallels and similarities that exist with trauma, timelessness, imagination, psychosis, and witchcraft and magick, and how the lines are crossed by all of them—with each other. It's actually both fascinating and alarming. Setting psychoanalysis, conjecture, and theory aside here, along with setting aside confusion, logic and reality, nobody will ever prove or disprove that the occurrences I described happened or didn't happen.

And *that* is what Magick does.

It confounds and defies the explainable.

When I left the courtroom, some media people who had witnessed my outburst earlier that day told me that I was going to lose for sure. None of them noticed the ashes being dispersed either. After I got home, I waited. My lawyers arrived at my house a bit later and said I had blown the case completely. They said the cards were stacked against me the whole time, and that now it was hopeless.

They had no idea.

I told them I knew they were wrong.

I didn't accept what they said. I knew better. I felt as though they were totally unaware of what I had done in front of them, or they were in some kind of strange denial. They were completely oblivious to what had

The Court Trial

happened when the absence of their linear clock time had occurred.

Or for the sake of skepticism, perhaps I was still in PTSD world, and I was in denial. But that denial was a magickal denial, a denial that they could never understand. A denial that can be turned inside out in another plane, a world of timelessness. A visit to a place of energy that cannot be seen by anyone outside of your own mind, and that is to your advantage.

A shocking thought raced through my mind. Maybe I never left my house when I did the ritual to invoke the Mother of Magick, and I had imagined the whole court scene, and that was why I was home now, and the lawyers just came to my house to see why I did not show up to the courthouse to testify.

Luckily, this was not the case.

I asked one of the lawyers what happened when I was on the stand, and he stared at me in confusion. So I asked him what happened when I got down off the stand, and he said, "Nothing happened." He kept saying that I blew it when I yelled at the lawyers for the Church, and that the damage I had caused may not be repairable. He had not seen the ashes scatter in the room. It was at that instant I realized that it truly did not make a difference if anyone else knew if magick activity had truly occurred or not—that this was not a movie set, and nobody was supposed to be watching to try to figure out what actually happened. But I couldn't help being curious.

So I pulled the bottle out of my pocket, and the bottle was in fact empty.

Perhaps it really was my imaginative travel that made me think that no one in the room saw the ashes disperse

A Witch Wins JUSTICE

from the bottle, and maybe I exaggerated the incident in my head out of confusion. But I had an overwhelming sense of victory, in spite of the lawyers' feelings of perceived failure. I thought about the bottle of ashes again. I just couldn't stop thinking about it.

Maybe I merely poured the ashes on the floor of the courtroom, instead of in the air, and I was lucky that no one saw me do it?

Such is the experience of trauma: the projector in your head playing back the scene jumps erratically, and the damaged film of memory tries to repair itself, while the absence of time allows the sequence of events to play confusing tricks on the mind in an attempt to defend the broken mechanism against further damage.

But whatever really happened in the courtroom, I did in fact bring the "charged" ashes into the courtroom in the bottle, I did pour them out in the courtroom at some point, and when I left the courtroom, the ashes were gone and the bottle was empty. Somehow, someway, I had accomplished the task of dissipating the Magick ritual ashes in the courtroom, and I was waiting for the consequences to take effect. It occurred to me that magick would only work this way. What happened in the courtroom with the convoluted time warping, and the disoriented scenes out of normal sequence and order, was the consequence. When a witch performs successful magick, the actual results are not seen instantly by the whole world, like they are seen instantly in a movie about witchcraft. They work in a way that makes people unsure of what really happened, and then the result comes as it was meant to and appears to be a natural result, without a grand showing of hocus pocus that

The Court Trial

someone with a video camera could post on the internet with clarity.

I was the only one who really knew that magick had occurred for a reason.

I went to the courthouse the next day, but I did not go inside. I saw several Salesian "people" for the church high-fiving each other at the coffee shop outside the courthouse and celebrating their victory, although the jury had not deliberated yet. The Salesians supporters and their crew were laughing and hugging.

I heard them say they have never done so well in a case before. They referred to their performance in the court as a "slam dunk."

No one said anything about the ashes I scattered in the air in front of them in the courtroom. The lawyers never noticed me even blink for a second, let alone go through the prolonged sequence of events I had experienced.

The jury was sent into the jury room to deliberate.

I went home and performed another ritual. Again I invoked the Mother of Magick, and again I burned more photos. I thanked Her for stopping time at the courthouse, still wondering if I were crazy to have witnessed the bizarre turn of events the day before; but whatever had happened, I decided to do the ritual again.

I felt compelled to repeat the mystical spreading of charged ashes while the jury was in deliberation, as I had the premonition it would affect the outcome dramatically. I took out a pen and a piece of paper, not knowing what to write, and I closed my eyes and wrote an incantation spell automatically, without even thinking of what to write on the paper.

A Witch Wins JUSTICE

Many witches and magickians believe in the power of "automatic writing" to create a spell to bind their enemies, or forces of darkness. I have done this before, and it is very interesting how words appear instantly in your mind when you have a strong intent, and usually the words come so quickly that you do not have to think of how they will sound, how they will look on paper, or how grammatically correct they are. The sole purpose is to use sincerity and intent to create the script for performance of magick. I read what I wrote and I felt it was meant to be used in the ritual as a binding of the lawyers of the church. I have to admit, the automatic writing surprised me, as it was unlike other spells I have written.

I read this incantation to the spirits of the distorted Saints who had been invoked and prayed to by the Pope, Cardinal, Bishop, and Salesian priests.

The Court Trial

As once you played with darkness,
you've cast your web of pain,
And prayed the Magick horror,
would leave without a stain.
Black blood you seep in darkness,
black lies you keep in mind,
The Witch you killed in terror,
returns with will to bind.
The candle burns your shadow;
your soul cannot escape,
The path you chose to darkness,
the lives you chose to rape.
No words you pay for can save you,
no lies you cast will slip,
Beyond the truth is vengeance,
black blood shall always drip.
Don Bosco's soul is tortured,
so innocent souls will find you,
As a Witch who charged the ashes,
with those ashes shall I bind you.

I wrapped the words of the spell around the photos of the Salesians, Don Bosco, and their lawyers, and I burned them in the cauldron. I poured the charged ashes back into the cobalt bottle and went back to spread more of the Magick ritual ash dust at the courthouse while the jury was in deliberation. This time I shook the ash out of the bottle at the door of the courtroom, and two church lawyers walked by me and passed right through the small cloud of dust unaffected; they did not see the ashes at all. I was still bewildered.

A Witch Wins JUSTICE

I assumed that they were so obsessed and consumed by the anticipation of the jury verdict that they could not see the ashes. But this time I was not in a traumatic state, and I clearly saw them walk through a cloud of magick ash, unaffected and unaware. I shook my head and walked away from yet another bizarre experience.

Then I went back home and waited. I did not want to be present for the verdict; something made me stay at home. My wife went into the courtroom and waited for the jury to come out. It took hours. The judge told the jury to answer several questions.

The questions were:

1. Was Mr. Piscitelli molested by Fr. Whelan?
2. Did Brother Sal witness it and not report it?
3. Are the Salesians responsible?
4. Is Fr. Whelan responsible?
5. Should Mr. Piscitelli be compensated?

When the jury came out, they answered the questions. They answered YES to every question.

I had won on all counts.

The Salesian priests and their lawyers almost fainted. They were dumbfounded. So was the judge. So were my own lawyers. So were the media. So were the court reporters. Mr. Mason took off his glasses and his jaw dropped. How could it possibly be? One priest cursed me loud enough for several witnesses to hear him. Another priest was crying.

The Court Trial

My beautiful wife walked up to Mr. Mason as he was in a daze and said, "Thank you" as calmly and as sarcastically as she was able to. She said he was bewildered and appeared to be in a stupor, as though he had been traumatized himself by an unbelievable occurrence.

A Salesian priest walked out of the room, and one of my friends who was there at the courthouse said there was some ash and dust on his black coat. He never saw it. We do not know how it got on his clothes. He was nowhere near where the ashes were dispersed.

I am not going to say I won the court case purely because of magick. I cannot prove that. What I will say is that the Pope, the Cardinal, the Bishop, the priests, and an untold number of Catholics prayed magick for Whelan, and invoked all of their saints and angels and their god; and they lost, and they are dumbfounded as to why.

I invoked the Mother of Magick and won.

What I can tell you is that dark magick consumes or "takes" energy from your body and somehow disperses that energy elsewhere, perhaps into the universe. I felt sapped. I felt as though I had burned thousands of calories or protein or sugar. Maybe it was all of the above. But I also felt psychologically drained. And I still cannot explain the incident in accurate detail concerning the dispersing of the ritual magick ashes, or what had actually taken place when I left the witness stand that day.

Those are the facts; you may believe what you will.

You may also believe or not believe that I practiced Black Magick, or plain magick, or no magick at all, and that I am quite insane. You can also choose to believe that I did not burn the pictures of the Salesian gang in

A Witch Wins JUSTICE

a ritual, that there were no ashes, and that I imagined the whole scene because I was suffering from delusional anxiety or whatever. Every reader "sees" or believes what he or she will, and the movie in your head created by the reading is your own concept of what occurred.

You can also choose to believe that my mission in this life was to change the outcome of a trial to a win against the church, as opposed to a loss in a church trial hundreds of years ago. You can also choose whether or not to believe in Karma.

Again, it doesn't matter.

The undeniable and legal fact remains: I won the court jury trial.

That is what matters.

But that was not the end of the court story.

The Salesian army of priests filed an appeal. "A priest cannot get a fair trial," they moaned to the press.

I believe that they may have filed the appeal because it was unacceptable to them that a witch could beat them in court, and it was unacceptable to them that after all the magickal prayers that were performed by the Pope and the Cardinal and all the Bishops and untold numbers of Salesians, that God would allow them to lose. It must have been a fluke. They had even been instrumental in choosing the conservative jury they wanted, and that may have confounded them.

After about a month, they got the results of their first appeal that they filed in the Contra Costa Court.

They lost the first Court appeal.

Perhaps they still could not accept the fact that a witch had won. No witch had ever beaten the Catholic Church in a jury trial in the US history, nor in world history

The Court Trial

for that matter, and perhaps they found this unacceptable. The Salesians kept appealing. Each time they filed an appeal, I performed ritual again and again, and their clergy prayed again and again. It was a game of witch versus clergy over and over again. The universe was inundated with energy of magick and counter magick repetitiously as the circus continued. I wore the victory proudly.

The Salesians filed another appeal in the California Appellate High Court. It took two more years for the appeal to finally reach the Appellate High Court. In the next two years it is probably uncountable how much more praying and magick the Catholic Church and the hierarchy did for Whelan.

I assume the Pope must have been exhausted and Cardinal Levada must have been boiling.

Just one word from Cardinal Levada would have stopped the Salesians in their tracks from filing another appeal. Perhaps he thought that this would be the final appeal that would sing victory for the Salesian molester and the Church; and that God works in strange ways sometimes, and they just had to wait a bit longer for their final victory in the State Supreme Appellate Court.

I realize that some people who read this will believe that the prayers not being answered by God for the Salesians and their hierarchy at the trial was predestined, and that God tests the faithful. Or, that justice was the cause that God was committed to, and the right thing was done in the jury trial, and "It was God's will."

I can understand this thinking, although I do not accept it at all. And I can also understand the counterargument. I think that many also believe that it is

A Witch Wins JUSTICE

probably a logical and scientific conclusion that prayer or magick is a waste of time. But millions of Catholics and Christians all over the world will still believe in prayer, no matter how many times it fails, and they will never think it is illogical and a waste of time or effort. But what do the Salesians think now?

Do they believe that it's true that magick or witchcraft is foolish and illogical? I can understand it is possible that they might. I also understand that when a result that is willed intentionally occurs, many people dismiss the outcome as luck or fate.

The true enigma is that the Catholic Church *does* believe in magick and witchcraft, although they believe it is the forces of evil at work; nonetheless, they believe in its existence. Do those believers think it now? Do the Salesians and the Catholic Church think that they were beaten by evil forces that outdid their own god?

There are so many questions that will never be answered.

It will never be known how the forces of prayer work against the forces of witchcraft or magick in the energy of the universe because of the invisible actions that take place. Although some scientists will still insist that the so-called "invisible force of the Craft" is invisible because it does not exist; then perhaps the very makeup of matter does not exist either. Maybe we are not here, and we are just assumed to be here.

An electron, which is part of an atom, is *assumed* to be there, because it too is not visible. Rather than continue to argue about invisible forces that are in effect in science, and how scientists know they are unable to explain various aspects of what happens when time

The Court Trial

stops, and how they cannot rationally explain certain other occurrences that confound them, I will rest that argument. I will agree with some scientists, and I will agree with many Catholics and Christians that witchcraft and magick does work.

Regardless of all these questions, I made an effigy of "Saint Don Bosco," the supposed founder of the Salesian order. I bound Bosco to a candle and did magick ritual to force his energy and his soul, if it did exist, to witness the horrors the Salesians have committed upon children throughout the world. I tied Bosco securely with rope twine, melted candle wax over him, and symbolically rendered him and his followers in a binding spell as useless to pray successfully for their case.

Whether or not Don Bosco was a child molester himself, I believe that his soul, if it exists, should be ashamed of the crimes he and the Salesian priests have committed, and that Don Bosco should join in commitment against the Salesian appeal.

He had no choice in the matter that day.

Therein lies the advantage to the invocation of the unknown world; it is defiant of arguments of rational conceivability, and comforting to those who do not care about the arguments, which are irrelevant.

Nevertheless, I took the binding effigy candle to Franklin Street in San Francisco, and dripped wax in the shape of a pentacle in front of the Salesian Provincial mansion. I invoked Aradia and the Mother of Magick to bind the Salesian priests, as before. I then went to Filbert Street in San Francisco, in front of St. Peter and Paul's

A Witch Wins JUSTICE

Cathedral, and did the same thing. I left the melting effigy of Saint Don Bosco at the church, with a pentacle around his neck.

He seemed to have disappeared into the atmosphere, I do not know what happened to the remainder of his figure, and no one has come forward with any comments.

Perhaps you may look at it as an amusing and fun expedition, or an unbalanced trip to San Francisco, to do weird things. Or perhaps you can look at it as though I am just plain an eccentric witch with peculiar ideas. Or perhaps I am insane, a result of having being molested and suffering from PTSD for so long.

Any conclusion suits me fine.

In August 2008, I repeated a ritual again when I received the date for the final appeal in my case to be heard in Los Angeles at the Appellate High Court. I burned the photos of the Pope, Cardinal Levada, and Salesian priests again, in yet another ritual at my home, and I brought the ashes I "charged" to the Supreme Court and released them into the atmosphere at the Court. There were three High Court Judges, and my wife and I sat in the very back of the courtroom to watch the proceeding.

The Salesians brought an army of lawyers to the High Appeals Court, and they had the floor to talk throughout most of the proceeding. The Salesian lawyers sat a few rows in front of me and did not notice any "charged" ashes in or around the courtroom at all. But the room was full of color.

This scenario was becoming all too familiar, and all too bizarre.

The Court Trial

They glanced back at me every once in a while, and one of them kept laughing at me. I do not know why. I assumed at the time that he was sure of a victory and that he was being vindictive. My one lawyer barely spoke to the three judges at all. We left the High Court room and talked to our lawyer for a few minutes in the lobby, and I said that I had to leave to go to the bathroom. When I got to the bathroom, there was a Salesian lawyer there, and I noticed he had some sort of ashes on the back of his coat.

There is no possible way that the ash I spread outside of the High Court could have traveled and landed on his coat. I went up to him as he washed his hands at the sink, and stared at the ash on his coat.

I was dumbfounded. It was the charged ashes I brought.

I shook my head, and he turned to look at me, wondering what I was staring at. It was awkward.

After two months went by, the judges made their decision. I got a notice from the lawyer. The three judges of the Appeals court had voted unanimously in my favor.

I won again.

Shortly after the appeals decision was decided in my favor, I wrote to the Pope, but I still have not received a response. I don't think I ever will.

He probably doesn't appreciate the fact that his prayers bombed for Fr. Whelan. Here is a copy of the letter I sent to the Pope.

A Witch Wins JUSTICE

Dear Mr. Ratzinger,

The last time I sent you a letter, you never responded. I know that Mr. Levada, the cardinal, sits at your side. Mr. Levada knows me very well, and he knows the filthy molester Mr. Whelan who abused me as a child. I know that you and Levada prayed for him, but your prayers didn't work.

I'm sure you know that the pervert who violated me lost in court, after you intentionally left him in ministry with kids, clear up to the verdict. I don't understand what you were thinking. Don't you feel bad that you did such a careless thing, to spite me and to use the kids at the parish as human guinea pigs?

You owe me an apology, and you owe all the parents of those kids an apology, for your carelessness. I think you should have more respect for children, and less sympathy for disgusting molesters who inundate the Catholic priesthood.

If there really is a Catholic god, I am sure that he thinks what your employees have done to innocent children is a disgrace. And he probably thinks you are disgraceful for praying for them. You should be ashamed of the vulgar, despicable conduct of all the unconscionable clergy that have ruined so many lives, without remorse.

Yours in Magick and Witchcraft,
Joey Piscitelli

I sent Bishop Allen Vigneron of Oakland a letter telling him I won the final appeal. Bishop Vigneron is the man who said the apology services in 2006 at all the churches

The Court Trial

and left my name out, and did not mention Fr. Whelan as a molester, to intentionally "snub" me. As I mentioned earlier, I was the one who had interrupted his crowded Church media event back in 2006, in front of hundreds of people. I had told him that he would always remember me.

I sent him a letter stating that all of his prayers for Whelan must have sucked, and that I had won the case. Vigneron sent my letter to the Oakland Police and tried to file a restraining order, saying that I "threatened him."

The Oakland Police contacted me, and asked why I threatened him. I told the police that I was a witch, that I had the right to freedom of speech. I told them that Vigneron was mad that I had made public appearances in Oakland at his Dioceses headquarters and had done numerous protests, and that it was my first amendment right to do so. The police dropped the case and did not pursue the claim for the sour Bishop, whose prayers had failed. Bishop Vigneron's spineless actions will have consequences, I am sure, as the energy he disperses is counterproductive to his own integrity.

Magickal Interference

I cannot prove exactly why the "power of Catholic prayer" and several million dollars worth of attorneys' fees and time did not win the case for the Salesians, Cardinal Levada, Pope Benedict, and their good buddies at the Vatican for the molester they tried to protect. But these are my speculations:

1) I do not believe that "God," if he exists, would condone the behavior of unconscionable child molesters.
2) The history of the Catholic Church in destroying innocents was due for consequences.
3) The people who "prayed for the molester to win" lacked sincere intent for "good."
4) The Magick performed by abusive clergy was for harm.
5) Begging a deity for an evil cause is antithetical to spirituality.
6) I was reincarnated for this cause, and Karma exists.

I don't think there will be anything remotely close to an agreement by any "experts" as to why I won the case and all the appeals. My own lawyers, who had told me the whole time that I would probably lose, would possibly say it was because of them that I won. That's OK. They can prove they are materially successful because they have lots of evidence supporting their success. I thank them sincerely, and I wish them well.

A Witch Wins JUSTICE

Some skeptics will say that there is no such thing as the "power of prayer," no such thing as "God," and no such thing as "Magick" and "Witchcraft." They will also say that winning in court is a roll of the dice—that "*luck*" went my way in the jury verdict, and the church and the Salesians were unlucky. These are all rational approaches and logical conclusions. They can also be considered scientific conclusions, in a sense, given the circumstances; you win some, you lose some.

As far as the rules of probability are concerned, given the lack of evidence I had for my court case, and given the historic outcome of similar cases in the conservative Contra Costa court I was in as far as the lack of evidence, the conservative pool of jurists in my county, the conduct I was ridiculed for in the courtroom by all the experts, and my lawyers' own convictions that I was probably going to lose, my chances of winning by a jury verdict on all the counts in the case were just about 0 percent.

The Salesians multi-million-dollar lawyers stated that the jury was unfair. I would imagine that many people and their lawyers who lose in court state the same thing. And that is why appeals are filed. The Salesian lawyers lost all the appeals, and none of the appeals judges were anti-Christian bigots. The same appellate judges who decided in my favor are also the same judges who ruled against other Salesian victims of abuse who had filed suits, and who tossed those victim claimants' court cases out in favor of the Catholic Church. So bias and prejudice can be eliminated.

That said, I would like to throw some fuel into the fire of skepticism and speculation both, by injecting some more controversial conclusions into the Cauldron of disagreements.

I myself, believe it or not, am a skeptic.

However, I am a selective skeptic.

I know that isn't fair, because skeptics in general will tell you that you are either a full-blown skeptic who does not believe in "God," Karma, and supernatural powers, or you are a believer. You cannot believe or not believe whenever it is convenient. They say that it does not work that way. Or, the same goes for magick, you either believe in magick, or you do not believe in magick. The same goes for witchcraft, or any of that "hocus pocus."

But as usual, and to light the spark of controversy again, I will bring up the theory of relativity and its salty result on the wounds of rational science. Because, as I have stated, I do believe in the theory of the transfer of energy, and I do believe in its tenets. With matter, energy, and time and space, things happen that confound science.

Accordingly, when you "stop time" and perform magick, you can be in two places at one time, and weirder things happen when you achieve this scientific state. As I have stated before, this state can be achieved by trance and PTSD, in addition to meditation and will. As Einstein stated, "time cannot be absolutely defined".

Here's something for skeptics to consider:

Some scientists say that Magick involving timelessness does not work; they do not know how to perform it because they do not believe in it. They cannot perform it regardless, because you have to have intent and sincerity for it to work. They cannot perform a magickal act involving timelessness by virtue of the fact that they do not believe they can. Reverse placebo, if you will.

They then conclude that magick does not exist.

This would be comparable to me trying to do a scientific experiment, and failing because I am not a scientist; I did the experiment wrong, because I did not know how to do it. Then, I would conclude that scientific experiments do not work, because my experiment did not work.

Therefore, according to this tweaked logic, science does not exist.

Today's scientific evidence may contradict yesterday's disbelief, or vice versa. The assumed disbelief in some types of magick of yesterday is often proved by the science of today.

Many scientists also say that "time" does not exist. This is useful, and the way you interpret this phenomenon can affect your ability to do mysterious things. And this factor, I believe, is one of the properties of magick. If you can ignore time, your perspective can cheat certain types of scientifical beliefs, and confuse arguments concerning the properties of time. And this is what I perceive that true magickians do; they access this realm by ritual means. They cheat science by using it, without its theoretical consent, and science contradicts itself.

We as human beings are made of the same minute particles of "energy" that the entire universe is made of: protons, neutrons, and electrons.

If you were able to control this energy, by any means at all, and you were capable of "playing" with time, you would be able to exist somewhere "else" at the same time that you were "here."

Magickal Interference

The Mother of Magick is universal energy.

No skeptic, or scientist, or anyone for that matter can prove that we are not made of energy. No skeptic, no scientist, or anyone for that matter can prove that the universe is not made of energy. Science prides itself on the fact that everything must be proven, and recurring tests must also prove the same result. It's a playground that keeps changing, but energy is always there somewhere.

The art of manipulating this energy, however, is another story.

How I Used Magick to Win the Case

I believe I won the case by invoking the Mother of Magick. And the Mother of Magick is inclusive of the laws of Karma. I participated in intentionally allowing it to happen, as it was designed to.

How this translates to my case, as simply as I can put it, is that I manipulated "energy" in the courtroom by will, because Karma was predestined for this case hundreds of years ago. Which in actuality, was seconds ago.

I believe that because I have practiced the art of magick with the inclusion of "energy" and the absence of time, and because I sincerely believe in the manipulation of energy and how it works, I achieved the desired outcome. Yes, this is also witchcraft, but it is the marriage of witchcraft with magick *and* science.

I do not believe I can manipulate the atomic particles in a plastic lotto ball, because it is not the same energy that is contained in a human brain, and I am unable to communicate with the atoms in a piece of plastic. Therefore I do not believe I can win the lotto with magick. I do not believe anyone can.

Unless Karma dictates the outcome beforehand.

`What is meant to be, *IS*.

But I do believe I can "psych" myself out enough in a ritual to communicate with my unconscious and have access to the energy in my mind. That energy is universal. It is capable of being in more than one place at one

A Witch Wins JUSTICE

time. It is a theory of science in addition to a theory of magick, which the church apparently cannot see, does not wish to see, and does not want to understand.

It is the same energy that is in the minds of the people on the jury, and it is the same energy that people utilize to make decisions.

Even if you think, dear reader, that my PTSD was what made me "travel" in the absence of time in the courtroom, that is all right with me. Because that PTSD was incorporated into the formula for the Magick occurring in the courtroom, as dictated by the law of Karma. In other words, if it was PTSD, it was supposed to be, because the outcome was predestined and it was part and parcel of that Magickal destiny. Likewise, that same PTSD travel, if that's what it was, is the product of the intended use of the Magick.

By using ritual and *symbols* such as ashes to communicate with my unconscious, I was able to "travel" in the courtroom and "communicate with the energy of the jurors," the energy of the universe, and my own energy to achieve the desired will. I will even go so far as to say that even if I was deluded at the trial, it was part of the magick, and it affected the jury's energy the way it was supposed to.

Again, let's go back to the skeptics.

They will tell you that this is nonsense, and that is okay. And I will tell the skeptics that the theory of relativity is magick itself, and that even after the theory was flaunted by Mr. Einstein, many did not believe that the magickal theory of relativity was possible. Many did not believe in Maxwell's theory of electromagnetism either. As stated before, science of today does confound science of

How I Used Magick to Win the Case

yesterday. And magick has always confounded logic and skepticism, and there will always be skepticism, and there will always be magick.

My claim is that I manipulated the energy by invoking the Mother of Magick, and the proof that my Magick worked is contained in the verdict in a case that I should have theoretically lost.

Ask the churches lawyers if this is correct.

They would never say that they lost a trial that they were absolutely sure they would win because of a witch who performed magick; they would scoff at the idea. They are rational, logical, and rich people. That is what matters most in life, isn't it?

Rational ideas, logic, and money.

They may tell you I was delusional and crazy, but that should have made it easier for them to win the case, not lose it. Right?

And I could not have won because I was delusional.

And conservative juries are not exceptionally prone to decide in favor of delusional kooks. That notion is inconceivable and not believable.

The only alternative for the church lawyers would be to say that I was **lucky**.

But that is what I want them to say.

Please say I was lucky.

I would be overjoyed if the lawyers said that I was lucky.

The *outcome of luck*, Mr. Lawyers and Mr. Clergy, is exactly what magick causes to happen. That outcome

A Witch Wins JUSTICE

is definitive of the process of intentional, true, and successful magick.

It's a win for me, whether or not they believe in magick, whether or not they believe it's luck, whether or not they believe I am delusional, or whether or not they just hate witches.

Any answers the church lawyers come up with are defiled and defied by magick and Karma. Because I won a case that they were sure I was going to lose.

The churches lawyers got paid for doing the work of darkness. But they didn't win. The church itself will replenish its bank accounts with daily donations, but they didn't win, not even with all their minions and all their cash. Maybe the lawyers don't even care, now that the molester priest was taken out of his position and was disgraced by a court defeat.

They received their "god" in their bank. Maybe it doesn't bother anybody in the church now.

It certainly doesn't bother me. I wear my victory proudly.

What matters to me is Karma, and the outcome that was destined to be. I have achieved the goal I desired, and I have achieved the goal that I was expected to several hundred years ago. Reincarnation, and Karma are a testament to the securing of deserved justice. Destiny and universal energy have made their way to the forefront.

I did not reincarnate and win because of my interest in money. That was not the lesson. The lesson, as explained earlier, was to learn, and to alter the outcome in this life to have a different outcome than what happened in the past life; and to seek justice from the organization

How I Used Magick to Win the Case

that caused the unfortunate experience of being killed as an innocent witch.

Many historians will tell you that the Church did not kill real witches: that there was no such thing as witches; that all the women and children who were tortured and burned were all people who were just unlucky, in the wrong place at the wrong time, and that they were not practitioners of any kind of witchcraft at all. I do imagine that there were people during the "burning times" who were killed for property, or because sadists were on a roll, or because some people mistakenly thought they were witches, or because of the hysteria, and the need for scapegoats for many different reasons.

But many were killed because they were wise men and women, or Pagan, or practitioners, or herbalist healers—in other words, some were witches.

I was one of them.

It doesn't matter to me whether or not a skeptic believes me. It has no significance in my life. Skeptics did not win my case for me. As a matter of fact, the laws of skepticism, if they were concrete and absolute, actually would have caused a loss for me in court, not a win.

I have already accomplished my role as a reincarnated witch, and that was to beat the church in a jury trial, but not just any jury trial—it had to be a trial for undeserved abuse. It had to be a trial wherein I was the underdog, the victim, and the unjustly victimized. It had to be a trial against the evils of the hypocrisy in the Roman Catholic Church.

It had to be a witch trial.

Destiny had the church lawyers bring the words "magick" and "witchcraft" into the court.

A Witch Wins JUSTICE

And this witch beat the church in a trial by jury.

I am the first in the United States but I won't be the last.

But it is my wish that other reincarnated witches seek justice, as Karma dictates.

No skeptic, or scientist, or anyone for that matter can take that victory away from me. No explanation, no rationalization, no spin doctor can remove that victory.

The Pope, the Church, Cardinal Levada, and the Salesians lost.

The Church lawyers got their money, which, if you break money down into the tiniest particle imaginable, is also made of atoms and energy. What I believe is that unfortunately, because that energy is what some people, and some clergy, regard as their "God," it will not be until later that they realize that the "Money God" is not a god at all. They will enjoy it for a short time in this linear life, and then they will die, not being able to take that energy of the particles of money with them to support them in any way into the universe after their death. No one escapes earthly death, and no money escapes earthly death.

It does not work that way, and it would be impossible to explain to them that money does not do anything for you after death, or in the lessons of life or spirituality or morality or right and wrong. This concept is not taught in clergy abuse lawyers school. I believe it is sad that that some church hierarchy and their lawyers are unwilling to see past the energy of money and do not concern themselves with accountability, nor does it seem that they believe in the concept of Karma. They can celebrate their love and adoration for money for a few more linear years, and perhaps it can be buried with them.

Although the clergy hierarchy who were personally responsible for the mass cover-ups and abuse cannot understand this, being devoid of true magick spirituality, it will probably not be important to them in this incarnation. Nor will the lesson of losing to a witch because of the law of cause and effect: Karma. This is nonsense and gibberish to them, as compared to stocks, bonds, property, and cash. But ironically, they will understand it shortly, as their clock time here on earth cannot be lengthened by any amount of their sacred money, and these types of people usually do not learn this lesson until the final curtain of life falls.

The worms crawl in, the worms crawl out.

Coffins containing the deceased, when lined with hundred-dollar bills, gold, and diamonds, are still are coffins containing the deceased.

I do not believe that the Pope or Levada or the Hierarchy believe in Karma either, as I believe they are concerned with the power of the Catholic Church, their sacred money, their molestation records, their supposed undeserved losses in court, and all manner of vulgarities. They still believe Eve led Adam down the path of sin, and they continue to despise women and children because of it.

I believe the hierarchy of the church is concerned with their accumulation of properties, art, and wealth, and the accumulation of people they can manipulate

A Witch Wins JUSTICE

to give them these treasures. They are concerned that the tradeoff where they provide faithful followers a ticket to heaven and immortality in the afterlife in exchange for material wealth in this life is always taken seriously by their followers. They are concerned more with their loss of money in future court settlements too, as this is a very important thing to the church—far more important than the lives they have destroyed by all of their rapes, tortures, and child abuse that they have historically shrugged off so easily for millennia.

I also do not believe that the church will ever accept the idea that I won the case because of Karma, magick, and witchcraft. I believe they will continue until they die to believe it was sheer luck, which ironically in my case is the direct result and effect of Karma, magick, and witchcraft.

Tattoo this in your head Cardinal Levada, and Pope Ratzinger :

MAGICK IS AS MAGICK DOES.

ACKNOWLEDGMENTS

To Linda, my beautiful wife of 32 years, who rode the roller coaster of PTSD, insomnia, ibs, anxiety, and depression with me for all those years; and offered her incredible support. To my children Sarena and James, and my son-in-law Brandon, for their perseverance and love. Thank you James for the original painting for my cover.

To my deceased Mommy –Chicky- who has witnessed the story from the cosmos; peace and magick always. To my father Sam, who clocked Brother Dan at Salesians for punching me out in class; in front of a cheering crowd.

To the Mother of Magick for assisting me in the victory over the causes of injustice condoned by the Catholic church hierarchy.

To Diana, Aradia, and the cosmos for the result of Karma.

To Attorney Jeff Anderson, the ultimate warrior, who has fought for justice for survivors and victims relentlessly without reservation, despite the bullets fired upon him by the powerful hierarchy of the RCC.

To Attorneys: Rick Simmons, Martin Jaspovich, Rob Waters, Kevin Shelly, David Drivon, Larry Drivon, for contributing to inevitable Karma.

To Attorneys Joe George, Cheryl Buchanan, Ray Boucher, Tony Demarco, John Manly, Mike Meadow, Tahira Khan Merrit, Erin Olson, and all the other warriors for stepping up to the plate for the unjustly tortured victims of the RCC.

A Witch Wins JUSTICE

To the genius authors Marci Hamilton, Ron Russell, Jason Berry, Richard Sipe, and Thomas Doyle, who stepped into timelessness to capture and reveal their stories;

I salute you.

To Augusta Wynn, for her advice, help, and time, and her Celtic beauty.

To news writer Karl Fischer of the Contra Costa Times, who started the ball rolling for me nearly a decade ago, with his story of facts.

To my Berkeley Therapist Dean Lobovits, for saving me from myself for so many years.

To Dr. Jim Jenkins, for his wisdom, ethics, honesty and support.

To Dr. James McCole, my doctor for 32 years, who knew how to treat an abuse victim such as I; with my multiple anxiety disorders, and PTSD. Thanks for your kindness, understanding and knowledge.

To internet truth seekers, for their courage and stories and postings; Frank Douglas,-Voice of the Desert, Alternet,-Witches for Justice, Pagan Space, Matt Abbott-Renew America, The Witches Voice-Pursuing equality for Pagans, Patrick Wall, John Deegan, Graham Wilmer, and Ken Kosiorek.

To local investigative reporters who are fearless; Dan Noyes, Ron Russell, Jeremy Herb, Rob Dennis, Aric Crabb, Matt Smith, Peter Jamison, John Simmerman, Dave Russo and many others.

To SNAP- The Survivors Network of those Abused by Priests, - David Clohessy, Barbara Blaine, Mary Grant, and Barbara Dorris, for supporting me, and allowing me to speak the truth at events to protect children.

Acknowledgments

To Joelle Casteix, for her beauty, brains, humor and inspiration.

To Terry Mckiernan and the staff at BishopAcountabilty, for their relentless efforts to educate the world on their website about accused and convicted molesters of the church; and to supply documents and facts to an uncountable amount of people.

To The Coven of the Purple Witch: anonymous pagan spiritual practitioners; who practiced the art of magick for the intention of the safety of children.

To those who protested at my side; Matt Hadden, Manuel Cisneros, Carol Mateaus, Linda, Dan McNevin, Wayne Presley, Frank L, Crystal Shaw, Nancy Sloan, Terrie Light, Tim Lennon, Ken Kosiorek, Mary Grant, Maureen, Augusta Wynn, Peggy and Dave Kamberg, Dominic, Ellen, Greg Tara, Dan and Michele Lopes, Brian, Jane, Melanie, Johnnie Pierce, and dozens of others.

To my dearest friends who have supported me: Lovey, Frank Lostanau, Dan Parks, Michele, and Marky.

To Jennifer Sapper, agent for the United States Department of Homeland Security, for her skills in prosecuting egregious clergy serial sexual offenders.

To my doggies Ralphy, Lola, and Mr. Baby, for their unconditional love.

To the following people and TV correspondents who have invited me to speak on their shows, documentaries, or contribute to interviews for written articles on clergy abuse:

Rick Giachino- Documentary-"Forgiving God" video 2011

Janice Edwards- Bay Area Vista TV show "SNAP"

A Witch Wins JUSTICE

God-talk- talk radio KGO Radio - SF
Oprah Winfrey – "200 Male Survivors" -2010 –Harpo Studios
San Francisco Mensa Intelligencer- "A Witch Beats Catholic Church" -2011
KCBS –San Francisco Radio
KRON - 4- Oakland
KTVU- 2- Oakland
KPIX-5 – San Francisco
KNTV- 11- San Jose
KTVN- Reno
NBC – Bay Area
KGO- 7- San Francisco
KCRA – 3- Sacramento
NPR_ Nation Public Radio- Berkeley Ca
SBNN –Santa Barbara News Network - video
News Channel -3 Eureka, Ca
News Reporters/authors:
Jason Berry -SF Magazine and "Render unto Rome"
Ron Russell- SF Weekly- "House of the Accused".
Jessica Agiurre-NBC.
Anna Kaplan-Stockton News.
Jeremy Herb, Rob Deniss, - "Abuse Was Common in Religious Orders"-
Guy Kovner- Santa Rosa Press Democrat.
Jennifer Garza- Sacramento Bee.
Dan Noyes- 'Man Accuses Priest of Molestation"
Eric Johnson -KRON TV
Sean Keohane – Clerical Whispers
Aric Crabb- Bay Area News Service
Laurie Goodstein- New York Times
Sam Shane -CBS Investigates – Sacramento News

Acknowledgments

Andy Blackman – BBC
Rita Williams – KTVU Oakland
Toni Earls – Irish Emigrant
Randi Shandobil- KICU News-10
Chris Metinko- Contra Costa Times "Victim Wins"
Trey Bundy- Bay Citizen
Keith Reid – Stockton Record
Cathy Hayes- Irish Central
Mathai Kuruvila- San Francisco Chronicle
Matthew Artz and Chris De Benedetti – San Jose Mercury News-"Sins Secrets"
Sheila Sanchez- Los Gatos Patch

I would like to thank the Police Departments of the following cities I have protested and held events in; who never attempted to stop me, and in many cases actually supported and thanked my fellow advocates and I; for our fight against the child molesters of the Roman Catholic Church:

Police Dept. Cities of : Antioch, Alamo, Alameda, Albany, Aptos, Berkeley, Brisbane, Benecia, Brentwood, Burlingame, Carson City, Chico, Clayton, Concord, Daly City, Danville, Dublin, El Cerrito, El Sobrante, Emeryville, Eureka, Fairfield, Foster City, Fremont, Fresno, Hayward, Healdsberg, Hercules, Kentfield, Lafayette, Livermore, Los Angeles, Los Gatos, Martinez, Marysville, Menlo Park, Mill Valley, Millbrae, Modesto, Montclair, Moraga, Napa, Newark, Oakland, Oakley, Orinda, Oroville, Pacifica, Palo Alto, Petaluma, Piedmont, Pinole, Pittsburg, Pleasant Hill, Pleasanton, Redding, Redwood City, Reno, Richmond, Rohnert Park, Ross, Sacramento, San Anselmo, San Bruno, San Carlos, San Francisco, San Jose, San Leandro,

A Witch Wins JUSTICE

San Mateo, San Pablo, San Rafael, San Ramon, Santa Rosa, Sparks, Sausalito, Sebastopol, Sonoma, South San Francisco, Stockton, Tracy, Vacaville, Vallejo, Walnut Creek, Watsonville, West Windsor, Woodside, Sacramento, Yuba City.

REFERENCES

I have taken the unconventional approach of not including footnotes and endnotes throughout the book, as the story is an autobiography, and the main subject matter does not require an extensive explanation of independent proof. The story can be considered a personal rendition and/or opinion of my prior life, and present life.

The sections of the book concerning the trial, and appeals court proceedings, however, can be verified by the actual recorded videos and written transcripts of the trial and appeals, which are available as public documents at the appropriate courts I will mention and list.

For those who would like to research the validity of my claims of press events, public appearances, and conduct as an advocate of children who were abused, there are numerous news sources mentioned in the Acknowledgments.

For those who would like to explore the mention and/or validity of the sordid activities of the Salesian Society outside the scope of personal experiences and activities I have mentioned in this book, there are numerous articles plastered all over the internet on various search engines.

Many of the articles condemning the behavior of the Salesian Society you will find on the internet may be stories and articles I have penned myself. Official Reports concerning the claims of molestation against the nest of

A Witch Wins JUSTICE

child sexual abusers who lived at the Salesian High School mansion residence in Richmond, California, are located at the Richmond Police Department. Other reports are located at the San Francisco Police Department, Los Angeles Police Dept, and several others.

The references listed below contain information that can be obtained on the internet, or at the courts mentioned. They can also be obtained at the archives of many of the news services who printed the articles concerning many of the Salesian cases; in addition to my lawsuit against the Salesian Society Order, and the Catholic Church.

(1) Salesian Br. Sal Billante's Victim Commits Suicide- SF Examiner 4-24-94
(2) Salesian Fr. Bernard Dabbenne Convicted - SF Chronicle 2-2-01
(3) San Francisco Weekly -House of the Accused- Ron Russell
(4) San Francisco Weekly- Blind Eye unto the Holy See- Ron Russell

(5) Superior Court of the State of California case: RG 03 104174: July 2003
John Doe 17 (Joey Piscitelli) vs. the Roman Catholic Bishop /Salesians of St. John Bosco
a) Deposition of Joey Piscitelli
b) Deposition of Anthony Piscitelli
c) Deposition of Vincent Piscitelli
d) Deposition of Linda Piscitelli
e) Deposition of Cookie Gambucci

References

f) Deposition of Dr. James McCole
g) Deposition of Rose McCraw
h) Deposition of Dr. Lobovits
i) Deposition of Bro. Sal Billante
j) Deposition of Fr. Steven Whelan
j) Deposition of Fr.David Purdy
k) Deposition of Dr. Arnow

(6) Report of continuous sex abuse by Fr.Stephen Whelan on a minor-(Joey Piscitelli) – Richmond Police Department- 2003

(7) Contra Costa Times 7-2-2003 Man Accuses Salesian Priest of Abuse- Karl Fischer

(8) California Appellate Court - Court of Appeal - 2nd District- Division 8
PISCITELLI v. SALESIAN SOCIETY
Joseph PISCITELLI, Plaintiff and Respondent, v. SALESIAN SOCIETY, Defendant and Appellant. B195450. No. – August 20, 2008

(9) http://www.richardsipe.com/reports/sipe_report_XX.htm
Appellate Court Rules Against Salesians

The authors mentioned further below are but just a few of the writers whose books I have read in my library. The opinions of the writers and/or their books are for reference only; I agree with some of the content in them, and I disagree with other content and opinions and/or stories they have provided.

A Witch Wins JUSTICE

(10) "Aradia- Gospel of the Witches" – Charles Leland -1897
(11) "The Mother of Magick"- Strega Viola – 1969
(12) The library of the "Coven of the Purple Witch" ; 3000 + books on magick, occultism, religion, science, energy, reincarnation, witches, witchcraft, stregheria, cabala, atheism, goddesses, atomic theory, relativity, bible, christianity, voodoo.

(14) Authors: Albert Einstein, Carl Jung, Steven Hawking, Charles Leland, Strega Viola, Nikola Tesla, James Maxwell, Isaac Newton, Isaac Asimov, Richard Dawkins, Edgar Allen Poe, Raven Grimassi, Sigmund Freud, Thomas Jefferson, Benjamin Franklin, Thomas Edison, Scott Cunningham, Richard Sipe, Isaac Bonewits, Jason Berry, Ron Russell, Laurie Cabot, Tom Doyle, Christopher Hitchens, David Mills, Starhawk, Patrick Wall, Sam Harris, Bertrand Russell, Aleister Crowley, Marie Laveau, Dr. Leo Martello, Arthur Waite, Dr. David Eller, H. G. Wells, Doreen Valienti, H.P. Lovecraft, Henry Agrippa, L. W. de Laurence, Brian Weiss.

Made in the USA
Charleston, SC
06 April 2012